Transforming
City Schools Through Art

Transforming
City Schools Through Art

Approaches to
Meaningful K-12 Learning

EDITED BY

Karen Hutzel
Flávia M. C. Bastos
Kim Cosier

TEACHERS COLLEGE PRESS

Teachers College, Columbia University
New York and London

National Art Education Association
Reston, Virginia

KH

Published simultaneously by Teachers College Press, 1234 Amsterdam Avenue, New York, NY 10027 and The National Art Education Association, 1806 Robert Fulton Drive, Suite 300, Reston, VA 20191

Photo credits:

Figure 5.1 by Noeli Batista
Figure 9.1 by Alycia Mecoli
Figure 9.2 by Marcus Moore
Figure 9.3 by Neena Massey
Figure 12.1 by James Haywood Rolling Jr.
Figure 13.1 by Erin Waldner
Figure 13.2 by Melanie Buffington

Library of Congress Cataloging-in-Publication Data

Transforming city schools through art : approaches to meaningful K-12 learning / edited by Karen Hutzel, Flavia M.C. Bastos, and Kim Cosier.
    p. cm.
    Includes bibliographical references and index.
    ISBN 978-0-8077-5292-0 (pbk. : alk. paper)—ISBN 978-0-8077-5293-7 (hardcover : alk. paper)
    1. Art—Study and teaching—United States.   2. School improvement programs—United States.
3. Education, Urban—United States.   4. Arts and society—United States.   5. Public art—United
States.   I. Hutzel, Karen.   II. Bastos, Flavia M.C.   III. Cosier, Kim.
    NX280.T75 2012
    700.71—dc23

                                                                                   2011046227

ISBN 978-0-8077-5292-0 (paperback)
ISBN 978-0-8077-5293-7 (hardcover)

Printed on acid-free paper

Manufactured in the United States of America

19   18   17   16   15   14   13   12   8   7   6   5   4   3   2   1

5/1/13

Contents

Acknowledgments

From the Editors: This book began as a dialogue about asset-based urban art education among the three of us, Flávia M. C. Bastos, Kim Cosier, and Karen Hutzel. Emerging from this project after working on it together for several years, we are happy to report that we still hold one another in high regard. As collaborative editors and contributors we wrote shared pieces, such as the book's Introduction and Conclusion, as well as individual parts. We each edited one of the three sections and produced individual chapters as contributions to our own sections. We have chosen a nonalphabetical order of authors for the book, listing Karen Hutzel first, to honor the leadership she has shown throughout the process. If it weren't for Karen shepherding the project forward, it might have wandered down an alley and gotten lost along the way.

Because this book represents a joint effort, we would first like to collaboratively thank several supporters of this 5-year project, followed by our individual and personal acknowledgments. We wish to recognize the dedication, flexibility, and meaningful contributions of the authors of this anthology: Sharif Bey, Bryna Bobick, Melanie Buffington, Clayton Funk, Olivia Gude, Leda Guimarães, Donalyn Heise, Carol Ng-He, Mindi Rhoades, James Haywood Rolling Jr., Kimberly Sheridan, Erin Waldner, Jessie L. Whitehead, and Kristien Zenkov. We would like to thank the Teachers College Press team, particularly Marie Ellen Larcada, Meg Hartmann, Aureliano Vázquez, Jr., the review board, and the rest of the team who have contributed to the production of the book. The team at Teachers College Press has been a tremendous pleasure to work with over these years. We also wish to thank Angela Mattox, our editorial assistant and graduate student at The Ohio State University, for quickly assuming the challenging task of compiling the manuscript and accompaniments. Finally, we also wish to thank our fellow (art) educators who have dedicated themselves to teaching in city schools and recognizing the value and creative spirit in their urban students.

Flávia M. C. Bastos: When I was 4 years old and struggled to learn the dance routines in ballet classes, my beloved teacher slowed things down and showed me the movements step-by-step. Being analytical-minded since then, I needed to understand how the movements morphed into each other and related to the music. Forty years later, as I reflect on this book project, I once again see the wisdom of slowing things down to recognize the support I encountered along the way.

I am thankful to my professional family at the University of Cincinnati, especially my just-retired Art Education Program chair, Dr. Robert Russell, who consistently stepped in so that I would be able to engage in scholarship and writing, while also providing cheer and a receptive ear; and Dean Robert Probst, who has been a passionate advocate for art education in the College of Design, Art, Architecture, and Planning where I work. My students also played a large role by reminding me with their intelligence, creativity, and unsullied enthusiasm that educational transformation is possible; and reassuring me with insistent questions and occasional admiring expressions that I have important things to say.

My dearest friend, Dr. Enid Zimmerman, listened to my early ramblings about this project, witnessed its development, and offered periodic counsel from the vantage points of former urban school student, renowned art educator, and caring mentor. My co-editors, Karen and Kim, have been sounding boards and admirable scholars whose work has inspired and moved me. Finally, I am truly indebted to my parents, Theresinha and Léo, who instilled in me the "can-do" attitude of a farm girl and a deep love of cities, and to my remarkable daughter, Amanda, who from age 10 to 17 has witnessed, understood, and valued my commitment to this project. My sincere thank-you.

Kim Cosier: I would like to thank my colleagues at the Peck School of the Arts at the University of Wisconsin-Milwaukee, particularly the faculty and staff of the Department of Art and Design, who are amazingly supportive of our work in art education. It is much appreciated. My newest UWM colleagues in art education, Rina Kundu and Christine Woywod, and my longtime pals Allen Caucutt and Nancy Mitchel make the good work we do together a joy. Thanks to my friend, colleague, and fellow rabble-rouser, Laura Trafí-Prats, for knowing and sharing so much. To my mentor, Enid Zimmerman, you will always ride shotgun. Also many thanks to my Indiana University "littermates," who are great mentors, teachers, and friends. Karen and Flávia, it has been remarkable working with you on this book—thanks! Your commitment to finding the positive, in places when so many others see only negative, is inspirational. I thank my mom and dad for teaching me to work hard and to give freely, without expectation. Finally, I wish to thank my wife, Josie, and her family (especially fellow art teacher and mother-in-law Fran) for giving me a home after many years without one.

Karen Hutzel: I wish to thank my many teachers, guides, and mentors, who have inspired and encouraged me. I cannot begin to name you all. I thank my students, young and old, who have had abilities beyond my expectations, challenged my thinking, and sought to make a difference. I thank my colleagues and support team at The Ohio State University for our shared mission of critical and socially just practices and research. Particularly, I want to thank department chair Patricia Stuhr for providing important support for this project; Vesta Daniel, for asking all the right questions when I sought advice, both professional and personal; and Sydney Walker, whom I can trust for her honesty and her belief in me. I want to thank my former advisor Tom Anderson, who believed in my abilities and taught me to do the same in my students. I thank Robert Russell, who upon beginning a doctoral program told me that it's not about how smart you are, but how persistent. I wish to thank my co-editors, Flávia Bastos and Kim Cosier, who have walked with me for the past 5 years in realizing a vision that began with a series of emails and phone conversations. I respect in each of you your commitment to seeing the good.

As a working-class kid, my parents taught me to do my personal best, work hard, never judge, and, most of all, be myself. I see these qualities in my stepdaughter, Brianna, whose passion, creativity, and energy inspire (and tire) me! Finally, I thank my husband, Ricky, for valuing flaws and encouraging me through the ups and downs.

Introduction

FLÁVIA M. C. BASTOS, KIM COSIER, AND KAREN HUTZEL

> Yes, one tendency in education today is to shape malleable young people to
> serve the needs of technology and the postindustrial society. However, there
> is another tendency that has to do with the growth of persons, with the
> education of persons to become different, to find their voices, and to play
> participatory and articulate parts in a community in the making. Encounters
> with the arts and activities in the domains of art can nurture the growth of
> persons who will reach out to one another as they seek clearings in their
> experience and try to be more ardently in the world.
>
> —Maxine Greene, *Releasing the Imagination*

> The current desiccated discourse on teaching and schooling needs urgently to
> be torn open, and sooner rather than later—bring on the artists!
>
> —William Ayers, *Teaching Toward Freedom*

Through this book we seek to tear open the "current desiccated discourse on teaching and schooling" by offering a vision of education through art. The approach we
envision is an imaginative process that holds the "prospect of discovery" (Greene,
1995, p. 133) and opportunities for connection among young people and teachers in urban schools. Education through art can create spaces for personal and
communal "be[ing] more ardently in the world" (Greene, 1995, p. 132), both il-
luminating and interrogating what is in order to create what is yet to be. Here we
argue for an education that matters, for a pedagogical stance that stands against
the tendency to shape young people to serve the needs of the status quo. We believe earnestly in opportunities for building community in each urban classroom
and every city neighborhood.

In *Teaching Toward Freedom*, William Ayers (2005) urges those interested in
transforming the discourse in education to look to "work[s] of the imagination"
(p. xii) to set loose "the energy of art to change people's lives" (p. xii). This book
is written in support of the kind of education only works of the imagination can

hope to accomplish. Like Ayers and Greene, we believe in the power of art to make the familiar strange and to expose hidden structures of injustice working against children and teachers in urban schools. Also, we believe that education modeled on artistic practice can help children and their teachers imagine a future where they and their cities are seen as assets, rather than merely as sites of danger and despair.

Contrary to conventional wisdom, which says that urban schools are failing and the only way to save them is to continue to do more of what has not worked over the past several decades, to test the life out of urban children, and turn away from things untested, we believe that urban schools can be saved only by turning toward things perhaps too complicated to be easily tested. As Eisner affirms:

> To suggest that education has something to be learned from the arts is to turn topsy-turvy the more typical view that the arts are basically sources of relief, ornamental activities intended to play second fiddle to the core educational subjects. Yet those interested in enhancing the process of education, both in and out of schools, have much to learn from the arts. Put simply, the arts can serve as a model for teaching the subjects we usually think of as academic. (Eisner, 2002, p. 196)

This book offers an antidote to faulty and reductionist assumptions plaguing popular discourse and informing policy regarding public education, both of which disproportionally and negatively affect urban schools. We look to art and the assets of the city to create models for an urban education able to break free of the current negativity and hopelessness we see before us. We believe that art can provide access to meaningful ways of knowing the complex world occupied by children and youth in urban schools. An education modeled on art can allow all those involved, children and adults alike, to explore their "urban imaginaries" (Huyssen, 2008), to see the complexity of what is while creating what can be.

This book encompasses our effort to articulate an alternate vision celebrating and capitalizing on the educational, cultural, community, and artistic possibilities of the city. Further, it articulates the integral and extensive role art can play in creating meaningful learning experiences across the disciplines. The contributing authors' art education practice and research provide a wealth of evidence on the affects art can have in the lives of diverse urban students. We are committed to overturn the usual talk of urban education as underprivileged, arguing that the educational promise the city holds to students extends beyond schools to include the rich and varied resources to be mined in cultural, communal, and artistic individuals, families, institutions, and organizations.

We examine and stretch Ayers's, Greene's, and Eisner's assertions that education should be modeled on art. We propose that quality urban education can be achieved by prioritizing art, and by building upon works of the imagination as a means to engage students in meaningful, relevant, and effective learning. Furthermore, we examine theory and methods supporting the role of art and visual culture education in a transformative educational process that sees urban students as critical cultural actors rather than passive and needy recipients of schooling. While we recognize the complementary and interdependent relationship among the various arts disciplines, in this book we focus on visual art. Here the term *art education* will be used as shorthand for a definition of an approach embedded in critical pedagogy, visual culture studies, and contemporary artistic practice.

URBAN ART EDUCATION IN CONTEXT

The growing disparity between urban and suburban school districts has been extensively documented (Kozol, 1991, 2005), revealing patterns of widening economic inequalities and segregation between urban and suburban school districts. The situation of a great number of urban school districts—a lack of certified teachers and high teacher turnover, a lack of basic resources, dilapidated buildings, shocking student dropout rates, and declining ethnic and economic diversity in the schools—leads to a common use of the term "urban" to mean, synonymously, underprivileged contexts primarily involving children of color. This contemporary corruption of the word "urban" contradicts the direction of art education development during most of the 20th century. Art education was born in the city and for most of the 20th century thrived in urban centers. Because of educational policy over the past several decades that narrowly focuses on reading and mathematics, however, the role of art in many urban schools has diminished, if not disappeared. Ironically, however, many of the urban schools that stand out as successful today have an arts focus.

A LEGACY OF EXCELLENCE IN URBAN ART EDUCATION

Despite the concerns and negative attention urban education draws from various segments of society today, there is evidence that urban schools have a history of distinction, especially in the area of art education. Numerous are the examples of school-based programs and curricula in the arts, underscoring the possibilities of art education in urban settings, including arts-based schools and distinguished arts programming.

Arts-Based Schools

Public schools of choice focusing on the arts thrive in urban settings. Being a "school choice" district, Milwaukee boasts a number of arts-based schools, including Elm Creative Arts Elementary School, Roosevelt and Lincoln Middle School of the Arts, and Milwaukee High School of the Arts. In Cincinnati, the School for the

Creative and Performing Arts (SCPA) has offered an environment since 1973 that enables the development of each student's artistic and academic potential, while providing incoming students (regardless of background, ethnicity, race, or gender) with the highest level of preprofessional arts, humanities, and sciences training available in the country (SCPA, n.d.). Many arts high schools, immortalized in the musical and TV series *Fame,* seek to promote academic and artistic excellence while also preparing students for postsecondary success in their selected artistic and academic fields. The Los Angeles County High School for the Arts embodies this philosophy and is proud of its integrated student body, including students from all socioeconomic levels whose reading scores are in the top 10% and math scores in the top 25% statewide. Students' arts-related accomplishments are no less significant, with graduating students being recruited by prestigious universities and arts institutes such as Julliard (Speer, Cohn, & Mitchell, 1991).

Many urban arts-based public high schools are recognized among the premier preprofessional arts training and college preparatory programs in the United States. They work with motivated and high-achieving students and their families. A study of parental involvement at Boston Arts Academy (Oumiette, Feldman, & Tung, 2006) demonstrates that an urban high school of choice is capable of engaging parents at high levels, despite the fact these parents come from populations typically considered difficult to engage. Furthermore, the experiences of past students, such as renowned art educator Enid Zimmerman, who attended a magnet music and art high school in New York City (M&A), underscore that interconnection between the visual art curriculum and the school's urban setting is integral to the learning experiences and accomplishments of students. According to Zimmerman:

> Going to M&A really saved my life. I was able to study art and academics with students from all over New York City and be exposed to the best teachers in the city. I still have friends from those days long ago. Being in the city afforded me opportunities such as showing an artwork in the Metropolitan Museum of Art, going on field trips to cultural centers and art museums throughout the city, and learning to be independent as I had to travel from the Bronx to Manhattan to go to school (an hour trip one-way). (personal communication, February 21, 2009)

Simpson (1995) also described two pockets of success she discovered in two Brooklyn schools. Both schools had art education programs with teachers committed to making a difference in their students' lives, which informed choices about how to teach art. Teachers design curricula that teach art while engaging students in making visual statements about the real issues in their everyday world: issues like AIDS, violence in the streets, drugs, and the students' own identity crises. Art and artists, both of their own and of other times and cultures, become known to the students through discussing them, writing about them, and producing visual social action statements. In this manner, art becomes a positive form of expression and a source of social, artistic, and narrative empowerment for the students. The experiences of these schools, briefly discussed here, illuminate the possibility of success in urban education initiatives carried out by qualified professionals and centered in the arts.

Distinguished Arts Programming

Many arts organizations and community centers have developed long-standing and well-respected arts education programs in a variety of arts disciplines (Burnaford, Aprill, & Weiss, 2001). In Cincinnati, not unlike other mid- to large-sized cities, the ballet, universities' music departments, museums, visual arts academies, and art departments offer enrichment, after-school, and preprofessional training programs for students whose ages range from early childhood to adulthood. In Milwaukee there are numerous arts-based organizations that work with schools, including programs at the Milwaukee Youth Symphony Orchestra, First Stage Theatre, and Ko Thi Dance Company. Visual arts-based organizations with connections to schools include the Milwaukee Art Museum, Walker's Point Center for the Arts, and an exciting new venture called Redline. In Ohio, the Ohio Arts Council boasts support from community-based and school-based arts education programs across the state, including CAPAcity, the Columbus Museum of Art, the Wexner Center for the Arts, Art in the Market, and the Kennedy Heights Arts Center, one of many neighborhood-based community arts centers located in Cincinnati.

The Kennedy Heights Arts Center was developed in 2000 by a group of residents who saved a historic building from being replaced by a storage facility by donating money toward the building's acquisition. With further support from the city for renovations, and numerous additional grants and donations, residents created an arts space that currently houses exhibition space, an artists' guild, and educational programs. The center's summer education program is founded on a commitment to community-based education, privileging the community's assets through exploration and investigation by a group of middle school students toward the development of collaborative and individual art. In the 3 years since the program's inception, evaluation data have shown a tremendous increase in students' and parents' sense of community and neighborhood pride. Such community-based arts programs serve as models of possibility in arts education programs that build on local culture and celebrate local assets.

Unfortunately, the excellence and high demand for these programs obfuscates the fact that by and large such distinguished programs serve the most privileged segments of the population and often attract suburban students to the city. For instance, even though the Kennedy Heights Arts Center is located in a community with an 80% low-income population and the program fee is minimal, youth participants are predominantly middle-class. There is also little relationship between the kind of programming in arts-based schools and the instructional and curricular activities that take place in the majority of traditional urban schools, undermining the potential for art education to offer a greater contribution to the education of urban youth. For every success story, there are even greater numbers of urban youth left without such life-enhancing educational experiences in and through art.

SIGNIFICANCE OF ART IN URBAN EDUCATION TODAY

Art and visual culture are an integral part of our vision of an equitable education. Unfortunately, the 21st century finds urban schools and quality art education to be nearly incompatible terms. While we offer several examples of arts education excellence in urban schools, they are sparse and tend to underscore a greater number of arts learning opportunities available to students at suburban schools (Stake, Bresler, & Mabry, 1991). According to Simpson (1995), arts education has nearly disappeared in many of our large cities, such as New York City, with the exception of programs in schools of choice or in a few other unique settings with outside funding.

> Arts educators have been struggling with the various constructs and conceptual strategies for urban education for decades. Failure to justify the existence of the arts in the curriculum is not uncommon in systems where law and order and the maintenance of basic curricula are the primary objectives. It is obvious that educational policy must change to meet the needs of the urban learner. . . . If the arts are to be part of that change, we need to make more definitive choices about how we approach urban, multiethnic students. These choices must go well beyond content selection and the recognition that art exists in other than Western civilizations. They must also reflect an awareness of the importance of the arts as a way of knowing about the world, as a way of making nonviolent statements about social and environmental problems, as a way of working cooperatively with one's fellow students, as a means of validating one's personal ideas, and as a way of gaining cognitive and technical skills that could help to break the poverty/disadvantaged cycle. (p. 29)

The lack of support for arts education in urban settings is a very tangible aspect of a well-engineered system dooming certain schools to failure. According to Duncan-Andrade and Morrell (2008), "Urban schools are not broken, they are doing exactly what they are designed to do" (p. 1). Perpetual school failure is tolerated because as a nation, we hold the belief that someone has to fail in school. There is also an economic justification for the educational failure of poor and non-white children, as schools are seen as a sorting mechanism in society. Comparing the different pedagogies and outcomes of the nation's schools, Kozol (1991) declares:

> Children in one set of schools are educated to be governors; children in the other set of schools are educated to be governed. The former are given the imaginative range to mobilize ideas for economic growth; the latter are provided with the discipline to do the narrow tasks the first group will prescribe. (p. 176)

In fact, the shutting out of the arts from schools is an integral part of the systemic disenfranchisement of certain groups by the school system. Furthermore, the general absence of attention to arts education in current educational discourse and practices perpetuates an ideology that disfavors the skills, critical engagement, and capabilities of students from certain backgrounds. The erosion of art in urban schools is not just a curricular issue, it is a matter of social justice. Children and youth in urban schools do not deserve the separate and unequal education they are too often receiving (Kozol, 2005). Secretary of Education Arne Duncan, from the Chicago Public Schools, described education in media interviews as "the civil rights issue of our generation." This book suggests arts education as a significant response toward civil rights by recognizing the potential of arts education informed by multicultural education and social reconstruction (Ballengee-Morris & Stuhr, 2001).

This book is divided into three sections, disclosing fundamental dimensions of our school renewal project: Part I, "Seeing the City: Resources, Assets, and Possibilities," lays out the theoretical underpinnings of our approach to urban education, drawing from community development methodologies and participatory action research. This first part presents a framework confronting issues of urban settings, without dismissing the unique needs and challenges of urban educators. It provides a discourse of hope and possibility, in which problems are met with creativity and the end goal of student learning and advancement is not sacrificed by oppressive understandings of urban students' potential. A broad understanding of visual art and visual culture that embraces the built environment of the city and schools is at the center of our vision of transformative visual art education practices in urban settings.

Part II, "Reimagining Art Teacher Education," outlines theoretical, philosophical, and practical implications for urban teacher education in art and visual culture. This part promotes the importance of an activist stance in urban arts education, which has been shown to be key to success in schools. The chapters in this part recognize the essential nature of urban teacher education in working for democracy and social justice and the power of learning through visual studies for urban students. Contributors showcase successful programs in teacher education and professional development and share knowledge gained through their important work in city schools and community and cultural organizations.

Part III, "Engaging Pedagogy: Curriculum and Methodologies for the City," offers pedagogies of possibility through application of teaching through an asset-based and art-infused foundation. Building on the previous two parts, this final part offers practical approaches and meaningful success stories of school reform through curriculum development and educational practices rooted in constructivist learning and cultural relevance, and considerate of local issues and concerns. Chapters will highlight successful arts and visual culture curricula and programs in schools and community settings that utilize students' and communities' assets and resources while building on local cultural dynamics manifested through art and visual culture.

This book unveils the possibilities of the city and the potential of urban school children for learning in and through art. We are inspired by the history of urban art education and look back upon the parts of our history we can draw from to create a more just future. We believe that Dewey's union of school and neighborhood, coupled with the notion of uniting "in one concurrent fact the unfolding of the inner life and the ordered development of material conditions" (Efland, 1990, p. 170), is a starting place for art education for social justice. We are inspired, also, by accounts of teachers who respond to the rich socio-cultural identities of urban youth and schools to create and sustain a sense of community through the arts. We are also inspired by artists who work in collaboration with schools and/or communities to engage in projects that change the face of communities and participants. We propose a framework in which schools can make a difference in students' lives based on the central role of art as a content and methodology for interacting with our immediate world, in this case the "community in the making" (Greene, 1995, p. 132) lying within each urban classroom and every city neighborhood.

REFERENCES

Ayers, W. (2005). *Teaching toward freedom: Moral commitment and ethical action in the classroom*. Boston: Beason Press.

Ballengee-Morris, C., & Stuhr, P. (2001). Multicultural art and visual cultural education in a changing world. *Art Education, 34*(4), 6–13.

Burnaford, G., Aprill, A., & Weiss, C. (2001). *Renaissance in the classroom: Arts integration and meaningful learning*. Mahwah, NJ: Erlbaum.

Duncan-Andrade, J. M. R., & Morrell, E. (2008). *The art of critical pedagogy; Possibilities for moving from theory to practice in urban schools*. New York: Peter Lang Publishing.

Efland, A. (1990). *A history of art education: Intellectual and social currents in teaching the visual arts*. New York: Teachers College Press.

Eisner, E. (2002). *The arts and the creation of mind*. New Haven, CT, and London: Yale University Press.

Greene, M. (1995). *Releasing the imagination: Essays on education, art, and social change*. San Francisco: Jossey-Bass.

Huyssen, A. (2008). *Other cities, other worlds: Urban imaginaries in the global age*. Durham, NC: Duke University Press.

Kozol, J. (1991). *Savage inequalities: Children in America's schools*. New York: HarperPerennial.

Kozol, J. (2005). *The shame of the nation: Restoration of apartheid schooling in America*. New York: Three Rivers Press.

Oumiette, M. Y., Feldman, J., & Tung, R. (2006). Collaborating for high school student success: A case study of parent engagement at Boston Arts Academy. *School Community Journal, 16*(2), 91–114.

SCPA Mission Statement. (n.d.). http://scpa.cps-k12.org/about/factsheet.html.

Simpson, J. (1995). Choices for urban art education. *Arts Education Policy Review, 96*(6), 27–31.

Speer, G. C., Kohn, K. C., & Mitchell, L. K. (1991). A public school of choice: The Los Angeles County High School for the Arts. *Educational Leadership*, December, 1991. Association for Supervision and Curriculum Development.

Stake, R., Bresler, L., & Mabry, L. (1991). *Custom and cherishing: The arts in elementary schools.* Council for Research in Music Education, Urbana-Champaign, IL. National Arts Education Research Center, University of Illinois.

Part I

Seeing the City:
Resources, Assets, and Possibilities

FLÁVIA M. C. BASTOS

> To rewrite the imagination in the service of a new critical imaginary—
> to provoke free and imaginative thinking—we must find ways
> to challenge the hegemony of realism, to engage the improbable
> through transgressive acts of imagination.
> —Eric Weiner, Chapter 2, this volume

This part is devoted to envisioning urban art education as the terrain of hope and possibility. In the context of the 21st-century United States, urban schools came to represent the substance of nightmares—part of a systematically dilapidated educational system that denies the promise of and avoids its responsibility to educate generations of youth. There are many educators like us, folks who are, have been, or will be in the trenches working with pupils, preparing future educators, or advancing practicing teachers. We share a vision, sometimes a blurred one, of a new urban school that makes a positive difference. I see city schools as laboratories of teaching and learning, places of exploration, excitement, and scholarship. My educational imagination is fueled by my own experiences and witnessed evidence in various countries of excellence in urban education. Anecdotally, I can say that the unifying forces driving such brilliance, often in environments deemed underprivileged, are insightful and competent educators who take inventory and advantage of their circumstances, honor the knowledge and experiences of their pupils, and infuse learning with creativity and the arts. This part honors these educators and draws upon their successes to propose a theoretical framework for advancing urban education that considers the city as an ideal site for learning about and with the arts.

Collectively, the contributors to this section describe and examine approaches that seek to reimagine education through the arts, and in particular through visual art. The goal of this part is to outline a pragmatic theoretical foundation to support this kind of work and to advance scholarship and research in the area of urban art education. The need for a theoretical foundation for urban art education is at least twofold. First, no pedagogy can survive or be effective if it lacks the systematization, refinement, and refocusing that a theoretical lens provides. Second, many texts focusing on urban education neglect to discuss or even mention the arts, as if art education bears no significance to the lives of urban students.

The contributors to this part draw upon the riches of cities. Without dismissing the unique needs and challenges faced by city educators, they articulate a discourse of transformation in which problems are met with creativity and the end goal of student learning and advancement is not sacrificed by oppressive understandings of urban students' potential. School systems shaped by decades of patterns of segregation and pockets of privilege led to a situation in which urban schools are the ultimate frontier. With four out of five Americans living in urban areas, urban schools' conditions and efficacy (or lack thereof) matter to us all. The approach imagined here draws upon a broad understanding of visual art and visual culture that embraces the built environment and the possibilities of city to recharge urban education.

In the opening chapter, I argue that high-quality urban education is central to creating sustainable cities and conceives of a critical role for art education in reenvisioning public city schools. Clayton Funk then examines women's long tradition of activism in steering and sometimes resisting the direction of administrative decisions about art and culture in public schools. Jessie L. Whitehead focuses on the tenets and process of counter-storytelling as a lens to examine the biases of urban education, and an approach to revise curricula and school art practices to honor the multiple voices of urban students. The three chapters in this part are keen in identifying the assets and possibilities of a transformative city education. They delineate powerful visions with educators daring to engage in defying acts of imagination that land visual art and education practices in urban settings as a privileged space of negotiation and change.

REFERENCE

Weiner, E. J. (2007). Critical pedagogy and the crisis of imagination. In P. McLaren & J. L. Kinche-loe (Eds.), *Critical pedagogy: Where are we now?* (pp. 57–77). New York: Peter Lang.

I

Artful Cityscapes

Transforming Urban Education with Art

FLÁVIA M. C. BASTOS

> We plan in reality to change the "face" of our schools....We dream of an
> effective public-school system that will be constructed step by step within
> a space of creativity. We dream of a democratic school system where one
> practices the pedagogy of the question,... [and] in teaching necessarily the
> content, one teaches also how to think critically.
> —Paulo Freire, *Pedagogy of the City*

> "Stay in line," "Keep your hands to yourself," "Be silent in the hallways." These
> ubiquitous commands in many urban schools are often printed in hallways
> and classroom signs, and harshly bellowed by teachers. The message is direct
> and violent. It implies expectations and assumptions about urban kids and the
> kind of education they deserve. In a Cincinnati government housing project
> where some of my art education students complete their student teaching
> experience, the environment of the school with its security glass windows,
> metal bars, and locked doors and a climate that emphasizes discipline
> and conformity establishes a poignant harmony with the hopelessness of
> unattended, cluttered yards and paper-covered windows of the nearby
> residences. A mere five miles away, I visit a brightly lit and vibrant school,
> where signs read: "Express yourself," "Have a wonderful day," and "Be creative."
> Colorful reproductions and original artworks adorn the public spaces. How
> can minimal differences in geography deliver me to such disparate universes?
> I am angry that these contradictions exist and are allowed to continue and
> outraged at current policies that sustain and exacerbate disparities. I am
> incensed that unlike me, most urban students are not free to travel the
> distance between demoralizing and inspiring educational experiences.
> —Flávia Bastos, student-teaching supervision field notes

What would it take to change prevalent narratives about urban education? How
can educators, scholars, researchers, and communities engage in successfully reimagining urban schools as sites of joyful, artful, and effective learning? What is at

stake when we radically consider the impact of urban schools in a society? These questions underscore a transformative framework for participating in personal, public, and professional debates concerning the possibilities of education in cities and the role of education in contributing to sustainable and socially just contemporary societies. This chapter has a twin focus. It assumes that (1) sustainable communities require vibrant, resourced, and interconnected educational systems, and (2) that artistic practices are effective catalysts in promoting meaningful relationships that result in articulating participants' voices, creating a sense of place and promoting opportunities for reflection and transformation in our cities.

Progressively, the term *urban* is less utilized as a geographical or physical location descriptor, and more often used as a social and cultural construct pertaining to certain people and places, particularly poor and nonwhite (Noguera, 2003). In the United States, for example, the majority of students attending city schools are underserved children of color. They find themselves in an environment that is prone to greater levels of regimentation more commonly associated with high-control institutions, such as penitentiaries. Activist scholars vociferously denounce this school-to-prison pipeline as the result of schools' increased militarization and regimentation (Lipman, 2006), and identify as primary targets underresourced schools and districts where students have "inadequate exposure to the arts" (Kim, Losen, & Hewitt, 2010).

As educators develop metaphors to better understand our practices (Jeffers, 1990), we notice that a rhetoric of education as scientific intervention, intended to shape and model students into externally determined end products, bears more affinity to urban school practices than, for example, a growth metaphor that considers the student/child as a plant or flower and the teacher and school as a garden. In this more bucolic, agrarian, and child-centered view (Scheffler, 1965), students are nurtured so that their potentialities may blossom, with teachers and schools providing optimal conditions to nurture and assist without much interference with natural development. In fact, many serious issues in contemporary education relate to the prevalence of an industrial, mechanistic, and quasi-scientific model indiscriminately applied to contemporary postindustrial contexts. Many educational developments, policies, and strategies still in use today originated in response to the educational needs of preparing skilled workers for factories at the turn of the past century. However, as Sir Ken Robinson advocates, in order to find answers to today's problems, contemporary society places a high premium on innovation, creativity, and the ability to articulate meaning from everyday experiences (cited in Azzam, 2009). Unfortunately, these competencies ordinarily take a back seat in public urban education. Therefore, the divide between students who received enriching educational experiences that honor complex skills and abilities, such as those associated with the arts, and students who suffer the increasing standardization and regimentation of public schools grows every day. This gap affirms education's role as society's sorting device.

With sophisticated and generally unchallenged justifications, educational policies and practices disproportionately affect urban schools, perpetuating ongoing struggles for cultural and economic justice (Buras, 2010). Typically, what we witness in urban schools is concentrated poverty; a student population made up of poor children of color served by mainstream, white, middle-class teachers; limited or lacking resources; and a dilapidated physical structure coupled with a complex and hard-to-navigate administrative apparatus. In common parlance, *urban schooling* is about hopelessness. Refusing to give up hope, in this chapter, I seek to lay out a persuasion for reimagining city schools as centers of educational excellence, catalysts of civic life, and cornerstones of dynamic cities enlivened by cultural and artistic activity. Confronting a bleak prospectus, this chapter will (1) describe how *Asset-Based Community Development* (ABCD) can provide a framework to better understand the possibilities of education in cities, (2) propose ways in which a place-based focus can guide practices and policies that will transform urban education and contribute to creating sustainable cities, and (3) reimagine through art education practices the role of cultural and educational institutions that have the potential to renew and sustain cities.

UNDERSTANDING THE EDUCATIONAL POTENTIAL OF CITIES: AN ASSET-BASED LENS

In recent years, *Asset-Based Community Development* (ABCD) has captured the interest of urban planners and community development practitioners in North America as an innovative strategy for community-driven development in urban neighborhoods and rural communities (Mathie & Cunningham, 2003). As an alternative approach, the appeal of ABCD (Kretzmann & McKnight, 1993) lies in its premise that people in communities can organize to drive the development process themselves by identifying and mobilizing existing (but often unrecognized) assets. In particular, ABCD draws attention to social assets: the particular talents of individuals, as well as the social capital inherent in the relationships that fuel local associations and informal networks. ABCD can provide a new lens to examine the challenges and possibilities of urban education.

In Cincinnati, I have utilized tenets of ABCD in my work with urban teens in the Art in the Market (AITM) Program, a university-community partnership that guides college students and urban teens in a collaboration with the Over-the-Rhine neighborhood, an underprivileged community adjacent to the University of Cincinnati in the creation and execution of public works of art (Bastos, 2006, 2007; Bastos & Hutzel, 2004). Tangible dimensions of the program include more than 50 artworks created and the community's strong sense of stewardship of them evidenced in the ways in which they have been preserved, never defaced or damaged. Less tangible outcomes relate to the program's ongoing 14-year history and the kinds of transformative experiences it promotes for college students, teens, and the local community. In addition to celebrating the physical and human assets of the Over-the-Rhine neighborhood, AITM established itself as a community asset, impacting the lives of youths, community residents, and university students. By gaining real-world professional, social, and artistic skills, and developing reciprocal positive relationships, University of Cincinnati students and local youth used art to change some of the images in that community ("UC Artists," 2004). I consider this evidence of the dramatic role art can play in urban and educational renewal and of the transformative potential of ABCD to encourage active citizenship in the sense of citizen-to-citizen ties, while simultaneously strengthening the capacity of people as citizens to better understand and claim their rights of access to assets, including education.

The language of many experts, mass media, and regular folks reflects views of urban schools as less than their suburban counterparts, with blame for the deficit laid in the laps of the teachers and students who inhabit urban schools. Discourse, practices, and policies target perceived urban school needs and seek to address students' deficits, underscoring the damaging effects of an overreliance on needs, instead of assets. An ABCD approach to urban education rests on the principle that recognition of strengths and assets is more likely to inspire positive action for change in a community. Coupling the identification of cultural, artistic, physical, and natural assets available in cities with the development of core associations, both formal and informal, with community members (Greene, 2000) can open up countless new possibilities for urban education. Research demonstrates that this kind of *education organizing*[1] (Gold, Simon, Mundell, & Brown, 2004) improves urban schools and underprivileged neighborhoods. According to Glickman and Scally's (2008) study, education organizing can effectively improve schooling by connecting communities and schools, boosting student learning, and improving the general condition of inner-city neighborhoods. Educational organizing strategies and their record of success underscore that schools and their surrounding communities are assets upon which to empower and renew cities. Teachers, school administrators, and community members are capable of working together to create the conditions of a transformative, equitable, and robust education. This hopeful vision for the future of urban education combines successful ABCD strategies and draws upon memory and imagination to achieve:

> the transformation of a culture from one that sees itself in largely negative terms—and therefore is inclined to become locked in its own negative construction of itself—to one that sees itself as having within it the capacity to enrich and enhance the quality of life of all its stakeholders. (Elliott, 1999, p. 12, emphasis in the original)

Therefore, we are invited to be inspired by Dewey's attempts at the University of Chicago Laboratory School (established in 1896) to integrate schooling with "the home and the neighborhood" (Efland, 1990, p. 169), and to ascribe a central place to art in developing students' expressive capacities, unveiling connections between practical and academic knowledge as a means "to feel the meaning of what one is doing and to rejoice in that meaning" (quoted in Mayhew & Edwards, 1936/1966, p. 341). Connecting past and future, art can be a powerful ally in re-imagining and transforming city schools and communities.

ENGENDERING PLACE-BASED POSSIBILITIES: A CITY EDUCATION IMAGINARY

What we think about a city, and our place in it, informs how we act. Huyssen (2008) describes an *urban imaginary* as "the cognitive and somatic image we carry within us of the places where we live, work, and play" (p. 3). Combining experiences and memories, urban imaginaries refer on the one hand to the way "city dwellers imagine their own city as the place of everyday life" (Huyssen, 2008, p. 3), inspiring traditions and continuities as well as disruptions. On the other hand, urban imaginaries also refer to encounters with other cities as a result of experiences that allow local and global to mix, such as through tourism, the Internet, diasporas or labor migrations, and television.

With over half of the world population living in cities, the challenges facing countries like Brazil, India, and the United States are increasingly similar, including addressing development and maintenance of transportation infrastructure; building and preserving safe, affordable housing connected to public transit; reducing crime and improving access to fresh food so that cities offer safe, healthy neighborhoods for families and children; and implementing environmentally sustainable solutions that create jobs while reducing our carbon footprint (World Urban Forum, 2010). While scholars in many disciplines seek to take advantage of an emerging knowledge about cities produced in the context of globalization, educators have also examined the challenges and potential of urban education. We must ask, What is our contribution to the issues facing cities worldwide? How could education become vital in supporting cities as vibrant, livable, and dynamic? Envisioning educational models simultaneously attuned to the needs and unprecedented possibilities of the 21st century involves paying close attention to the place-specific experiences we encounter in cities.

With the exception of a small number of "global" cities such as New York and Los Angeles, in the United States since the end of World War II cities have declined in importance as economic, political, and social centers (Noguera, 2003). A deeply ingrained belief that owning a home is the gateway to safer neighborhoods and better schools and its support system of incentives and subsidies pushes people to live in suburbs (Kiviat, 2010). This leaves urban cores vacant of substantial economic investment and results in a dilapidated infrastructure that creates zip codes predominantly inhabited by the disproportionately black and Latino urban poor. Working as a sophisticated form of redlining and adding insult to injury, poor schools also work against community improvement, contributing to the list of negatives (such as crime and substandard housing) that afflict many inner-city neighborhoods. Good schools, on the other hand, are important components of healthy, economically strong communities. They benefit the neighborhood, increasing its attractiveness to new families who seek advancement for their children and offering chances for upward mobility of current residents (Center for Community Change, 2005).

According to Giroux (1996), schooling has been redefined through a corporate ideology stressing the "primacy of choice over community, competition over cooperation, and excellence over equity" (p. ix). Intrinsic to these values are grandiose efforts to structure public schooling around the interrelated practices of competition, reprivatization, standardization, and individualism. Among these proposed remedies are dangerous policies such as No Child Left Behind (NCLB) (Chapman, 2007) and the 2009 federal government initiative Race to the Top, rewarding states that implement educational innovations and improvements (Race to the Top Fund, 2010). Ultimately, these strategies punish urban and inner-city schools that are hurting the most; focus almost exclusively on science, technology, and mathematics; and hinder dimensions of schooling that have greater potential to be meaningful to students—the areas of self-expression, creativity, and the arts.

Conversely, as Garnett (2010) points out, art and creativity are central to many urban development strategies that pin hopes of central city renewal on the *creative class* (Florida, 2002). This "cool cities" strategy is not unreasonable. A plausible case can be made that many downtown areas have experienced a rebound in recent years, fueled by a growing preference among elites for city life. Still, while many central cities' fortunes have improved during the last decade and a half, including the decline of concentrated poverty and the reverse of population losses, most cities continue to lose middle-class families even as they gain wealthier citizens. These newcomers tend not to have children who attend public schools, and thus overall urban health is diminished, especially with regard to the connection among homeownership, schools, and healthy and vibrant urban neighborhoods.

An urban imaginary inspired by Florida's (2005) views places cities as the prime location for the creative lifestyle and associated new amenities, even as systematic art education experiences gradually disappear from public schools. We witness cities all over the country benefiting from the energy and revenues provided by creative young professionals who stay single longer than in previous generations and who prefer to live in diverse, urban neighborhoods (Bruegman, 2005). However, as Kotkin (2005) argues, there are limits to the lure of hipness and coolness. In fact, while a handful of cities may find their sustenance as amusement parks for adults, the most successful cities focus on important but arguably *uncool* issues such as housing, education, family-sustaining employment, and public policy. I, therefore, propose a partnership between the artistic and creative assets germane to urban environments, and arts-focused education initiatives can engender a new and sound approach to urban education, with the potential to favorably impact the sustainability of cities. Addressing the concerns of many parents about the poor quality of urban schools and the implications for them, their children, and their decisions as parents to send their children there (Martin, 2008), I draw on historical and contemporary developments that honor the city as a prime educational and artistic site. In this book I hope to instigate our educational imagination to reconsider the possibilities of urban education, drawing on city assets, chiefly their artistic and creative dimensions, to create high quality schools (Sutton, 1996). I envision a city-based education in which a place-based focus can guide practices and policies that will transform urban education and contribute to creating sustainable cities through a rich partnership between urban art and schools.

REIMAGINING CITIES, ART, AND EDUCATION

In order to reimagine city education, we can (1) consider an expanded role for art, cultural, and education institutions in the transformation of city schools; (2) design art-infused education practices that have the potential to renew and sustain cities; and (3) entertain the rich possibilities of partnerships between urban schools and cities to offer the most exciting and meaningful educational opportunities for students.

As discussed in this chapter, teachers, administrators, students and their families, local media, and policymakers often dwell on the many resources school lack, the poor conditions of school buildings, and the violence shaping school life. While these negative dimensions of city schooling are widely and sharply documented (Kozol, 1991, 2005), fortunately there are counterexamples springing from innovative connections between art and education that are grounded in the specificity the city. For example, a magnet school in Los Angeles announces a new era in urban education according to Loh's (2008) experience as a parent unable to flee to white suburbs and to afford private schooling. Her daughters attended public school with the urban poor in a neighborhood where 80% of residents were Hispanic, a substantial portion of whom were recent arrivals. Her eldest daughter was the only blonde in her class of 20, her grade being about one-third English learners. In the district less than 9% of the students were white. She commented that for many families the aesthetics of urban schools alone were horrifying—the chain-link fence, putty-colored bungalows, fluorescent lighting, and, as one parent put it, "even the grass made me sad," and to another the kindergarten wall art looked "rote." Despite the aesthetic challenges and the general (middle-class white) public perception, there were significant things happening. At the high school, largely due to the involvement of Korean parents, graduates were headed to Harvard, Stanford, Yale, Cal Tech, and Berkeley. At the elementary school, in which 56 percent of the students were in free or reduced price lunch, the aesthetically uninspiring outside stood in opposition to a plethora of books, computers, LeapFrog pads, and the like because Title I schools with a substantial portion of low-income students are eligible for hundreds of thousands of federal dollars that affluent schools are not. According to Loh, the overall school climate was "probably helped by our wide mix of ethnicities—no one group overwhelms the school, so no minority feels disenfranchised" (p. 95). Capitalizing on the diverse cultural context of the city and the needs of families for better-quality education, the assets these families bring, existing school resources, and the existing policies and funding mechanisms produced these improvements.

Historically, art education developed in the United States in close connection with the resources, opportunities, and assets of cities. Museums, cultural institutions, and the sheer hubbub of people and events have created opportunities for exciting and current educational practices. Today many cities, whether cosmopolitan or mid-sized, still support a myriad of service organizations, arts centers, places of worship, universities, museums, and community centers that have education and outreach missions, many of which encompass the arts. Artists themselves also represent an important asset to cities and education. Beyond being representatives of the creative class—the visionary urban dwellers who see possibilities where middle-class suburbanites see blight—artists increasingly take on a huge role in community cultural development (Goldbard, 2006). Responding to current social conditions, many artists work with local communities to promote change.

Grounded in social critique and social imagination as inspired in the transformative pedagogy of Brazilian educator Paulo Freire (1982), artists frequently engage in a kind of community-based work that seeks to improve life conditions and empower residents of various communities. Many are the examples of these contemporary change agents: Lily Yeh's work in the Village of Art and Humanities in North Philadelphia resulted in a 10-square-block area where abandoned lots were reclaimed into gardens of low undulating walls, mosaics and wall murals surrounded by tiled courtyards, and trees growing in a community nursery; No Name Gallery in Minneapolis created a niche for emerging artists through substantial community organizing that transformed an abandoned riverfront gallery into a worthy arts space in one of the city's oldest neighborhoods; Clara Wainwright, a Boston-based public celebration artist and quilt-maker, founded the Faith Quilts Project, a collaborative project that brings people together to talk about faith as a critical issue to our collective welfare—participants representing some two dozen faith traditions as well as interfaith collaborations experience the combination of reflection, verbal exchange, and the creation of something expressive that allows for an examination of the value of faith in peoples' lives (Elizabeth & Young, 2006).

Many artists working in urban communities subscribe to a desire to "inhabit the world in a better way" (Bourriad, 2002, p. 13). Their practice and work bear much affinity to the kinds of community development and education organizing that can bring about change in cities and schools. Understanding the city as a community par excellence, artists model how creativity and imagination coupled with personal and local assets can support the creation and expansion of networks that can affect change. *Community* is not defined here in narrow middle-class terms (the neighborhood where one lives, goes to school, and interacts with neighbors of a shared social economic background). Community is understood broadly, as a fluid and expansive network of relationships, including the view that students in a particular community school are in fact connected to other schools by virtue of their associations. Community is understood as ecology, not a geographic location with set boundaries. Two central premises guide this chapter: (1) that a sustainable community is one that has a vibrant educational system that interconnects and shares resources among various schools, organizations, and institutions, and (2) that art—understood in broad terms—is a tremendous catalyst to create and support connections among the many players in a city environment, creating a sense of place and fostering opportunities for reflection and social change.

Collectively, cities, artists, and formal and informal organizations can work to create new understandings of and possibilities for urban education. Language, signs, and encounters organize our experiences with everyday life. If as educators we are able to transform our language about city schools and resignify our interpretations, shifting from needs and problems to focus on assets and possibilities, we can contribute to an unprecedented movement of renewal that can change city schools as we know them. To act on the promise of education in cities requires proposing remedies that build on existing assets and are expected to unleash schools' pivotal role in urban renewal. Sharing the vision of Brazilian educator Paulo Freire, who as Secretary of Sao Paulo's Bureau of Education, one of Latin America's largest cities, sought to "transform schools in creative centers, where one teaches and learns with joy" (1993, p. 28), educators can organize and advocate for the critically central role arts education can play in reenvisioning urban public schools. New ways to consider the issues facing urban schools through the application of principles of asset-based planning provide a perspective that regards the quality of urban education as central to creating sustainable and just urban communities. More importantly, art education, and an education inspired by contemporary art practices, can play a pivotal role in this renewal process. I invite readers to consider the possibilities outlined here as a means to expand our own collective imaginary about cities and schools and to more adequately respond to the pressing and timely issues of today. A high-quality urban education is central in creating sustainable cities because schools can be catalysts of democracy and excellence enhancing cities across the globe.

NOTE

1. Education organizing is a new branch of community organizing that seeks to make schools more responsive to community needs, advocating bottom-up changes and based on developing power and trust in urban neighborhoods (see the Collaborative for Education Organizing for further information: http://www.cfncr.org/site/c.ihLSJ5PLKuG/b.3562029/k.3BC/Collaborative_for_Education_Organizing.htm).

REFERENCES

Azzam, A. M. (2009). Why creativity: A conversation with Sir Ken Robinson. *Educational Leadership, 67*(1), 22–26.

Bastos, F. M. C. (2006). Enhancing life through learning: An examination of my service learning practice in art education. In R. K. Roy & M. Cho (Orgs.) *My art, my world: A handbook on integrating service learning into the art classroom* (pp. 6–9). Miami: Florida Learn and Serve.

Bastos, F. M. C. (2007). Art in the Market program: Ten years of community-based art education. *Journal of Cultural Research in Art Education, 25*, 51–63.

Bastos, F. M. C., & Hutzel, K. (2004). "Art in the Market" project: Addressing racial issues through community art. *Journal of Cultural Research in Art Education, 22*, 86–98.

Bourriard, N. (2002). *Relational aesthetics.* Les Presses Du Reel, France.

Bruegman, R. (2005). *Sprawl: A compact history.* Chicago: University of Chicago Press.

Buras, K. L. (2010). Counterstories on pedagogy and policy making: Coming of age in a privatized city. In K. L. Buras, J. Randels, K. Salaam, & Students at the Center, *Pedagogy, policy, and the privatized city: Stories of dispossession and defiance from New Orleans* (pp. 1–14). New York: Teachers College Press.

Center for Community Change. (2005). *An action guide for education organizing.* Washington, DC: Author.

Chapman, L. H. (2007). An update on No Child Left Behind and national trends in education. *Arts Education Policy Review, 109*(1), 25–36.

Collaborative for Education Organizing. http://www.cfncr.org/site/c.ihLSJ5PLKuG/b.3562029/k.3BC/Collaborative_for_Education_Organizing.htm.

Efland, A. (1990). *A history of art education: Intellectual and social currents in teaching the visual arts.* New York: Teachers College Press.

Elizabeth, L., & Young, S. (2006). *Works of heart: Building village through the Arts.* Oakland, CA: New Village Press.

Elliott, C. (1999). *Locating the energy for change: An introduction to appreciative inquiry.* Winnipeg: International Institute for Sustainable Development.

Florida, R. (2002). *The rise of the creative class: And how it's transforming work, leisure, community and everyday life.* New York: Basic Books.

Florida, R. (2005). *Cities and the creative class.* New York: Routledge.

Freire, P. (1982). *Pedagogy of the oppressed.* New York: Continuum.

Freire, P. (1993). *Pedagogy of the city.* New York: Continuum.

Garnett, N. S. (2010). Affordable private education and the middle class city. *The University of Chicago Law Review, 71*(202), 201–222.

Glickman, J., & Scally, C. P. (2008). Can community and education organizing improve inner-city schools? *Journal of Urban Affairs, 30*(5), 557–577.

Gold, E., Simon, E., Mundell, L., & Brown, C. (2004). Bringing community organizing into the school reform picture. *Nonprofit and Voluntary Sector Quarterly, 33*(1S), 54–77.

Goldbard, A. (2006). *New creative community: The art of cultural development.* Oakland, CA: New Village Press.

Greene, M. (2000). *The power of associations: Not mapping but organizing* (unpublished paper). ABCD Neighborhood Circle Initiative, ABCD Institute, Evanston, IL.

Huyssen, A. (Ed.). (2008). *Other cities, other worlds: Urban imaginaries in a globalizing age.* Durham, NC: Duke University Press.

Jeffers, C. S. (1990). Child-centered and discipline-based art education: Metaphors and meanings. *Art Education, 43*(2), 16–21.

Kim, C., Losen, P., & Hewitt, D. (2010). *The school-to-prison pipeline.* New York: New York University Press.

Kiviat, B. (2010). The case against home ownership. *Time Magazine, 176*(10), 40–46.

Kotkin, J. (2005, October). Uncool cities. *Prospect Magazine.* Retrieved from http://www.prospectmagazine.co.uk/2005/10/uncoolcities.

Kozol, J. (1991). *Savage inequalities: Children in America's schools.* New York: HarperPerennial.

Kozol, J. (2005). *The shame of the nation: Restoration of apartheid schooling in America.* New York: Three Rivers Press.

Kretzmann, J., & McKnight, J. (1993). *Building communities from the inside out.* Chicago: ACTA Publications.

Lipman, P. (2006). "This is America" 2005: The political economy of education reform against the public interest. In G. Ladson-Billings & W. Tate (Eds.), *Education research in the public interest* (pp. 98–118). New York: Teachers College Press.

Loh, S. T. (2008). Tales out of school. *The Atlantic, 301*(2), 91–97.

Martin, L. (2008). Boredom, drugs, and school: Protecting children in gentrifying communities. *City & Community, 7*(4), 331–346.

Mathie, A., & Cunningham, G. (2003). From clients to citizens: Asset-based Community Development as a strategy for community-driven development. *Development in Practice, 13*(5), 474–486.

Mayhew, K., & Edwards, A. (1966). *The Dewey school: The laboratory school at the University of Chicago.* New York: Appleton-Century Co. (Original work published 1936)

Noguera, P. A. (2003). *City schools and the American Dream: Reclaiming the promise of public education.* New York: Teachers College Press.

Race to the Top Fund. (2010). http://www2.ed.gov/programs/racetothetop/index.html.

Scheffler, I. (1965). *The language of education.* Springfield, IL: Charles Thomas.

Sutton, S. E. (1996). *Weaving a tapestry of resistance: The places, power, and poetry of a sustainable society.* Westport, CT: Bergin & Garvey.

UC artists work with city youths. (2004, May 26). *The Cincinnati Enquirer,* p. 3B.

World Urban Forum (2010). http://www.whitehouse.gov/blog/2010/03/25/world-urban-forum-2010-live-update.

2

The Business of Beauty

Women as Assets in the City Beautiful Movement

CLAYTON FUNK

> In a civilization that proposed to begin with a City on a Hill, we have learned
> a great deal about what happened to the hill but very little about what
> happened to the city.
>
> —Warren Susman, *Culture as History*

Women have a long tradition of advancing art education in urban schooling in
the United States. In contemporary art education and in the past, the activism of
women has steered and sometimes resisted the direction of administrative decisions about art and culture in public schools. Michelle Fine (1993), for example,
describes women active in late-20th-century schools in Chicago and in their communities: parents of Chicago Public Schools students are primary decisionmakers
in those schools, with intent to import "concerns of culture, class, and community
into their schools, as is obvious in the rise of interest in African-centered curricula, afterschool programs, and community-service schools" (Fine, 1993, p. 12).
Empowered as such, parents interrupt the power of "professionals." In a similar
way, during the early 20th century members of the Chicago Woman's Club (CWC)
worked to support Chicago neighborhood life and trouble the Chicago Board
of Education's (CBE) paradigm of scientific management with its class and race
bias. This chapter is, therefore, a lesson from history that shows that such cultural
and social networks did and still do affect art education in contemporary public
schooling.

The CWC contributed paintings, prints, sculptures, and other visual art forms
to Chicago's public vocational high schools, where the CBE had determined that
such "fine art education" was unnecessary, excluding working-class students from
art forms that educators believed would uplift and inspire good character (Bailey,
1914; Rohr, 2004). Specifically, the art forms introduced by CWC clubwomen into
vocational high schools were mural commissions by the CWC's Public School Art
Society (PSAS). I will discuss the mural projects for Chicago's Wendell Phillips

High School (WPHS), an all-male, racially integrated vocational high school. This narrative will also show how CWC clubwomen expanded their efforts into the community as they promoted and made innovations in the progression of mural-painting and identified social and racial relationships, turning them into assets of neighborhood life, thus breaking through templates of segregation imposed by professional planners and public officials. The work of the CWC clubwomen becomes a lesson for today's teachers and community workers as it reveals how clubwomen used assets—social and cultural opportunities and human potential—within Chicago neighborhoods to resist the status quo and help promote social reform.

The neighborhood work of the CWC was part of a larger context known as the City Beautiful Movement. Some historians (e.g., Condit, 1973; Manieri-Elia, 1980; Schlereth, 1992) have framed the "Chicago Plan" (also called the "Burnham Plan") as the beginning of the City Beautiful Movement, derived from the World's Columbian Exposition in 1893, which served as a model city for the Chicago Plan. At that time women were not at the forefront; mostly male officials from businesses and city government organized the Chicago Commercial Club for economic development to oversee development of the master plan. Chicago would be a centralized municipality surrounding an urban core of monumental buildings, wide streets, and parks in the Beaux Arts style. If the historians mentioned the CWC clubwomen at all, they usually described them as helpers to this "official" City Beautiful program. Telling the story another way, consider a history of City Beautiful about women activists whose work predated the Chicago Plan by decades. These women acted not as "helpers" but followed their own social compasses (e.g., Szczygiel, 2003; Wilson, 1989). Such women activists—Jane Addams and Ellen Gates Starr leaders among them—believed they would be more effective working on the street level in neighborhoods than if they followed the scientifically uniform templates for neighborhood life designed by aloof professional planners. This chapter is about those women activists in the CWC and how they established a tradition of clubwomen working in public schools that is still practiced today.

CWC CLUBWOMEN, SCHOOL ADMINISTRATORS, AND SOCIAL CLOSURE

When CWC clubwomen advocated for art education, they weighed into the political territory of the CBE. In doing so, they reversed their exclusion from influencing CBE educational policy, bringing with them the voices of public school teachers as well. According to Raymond Murphy, acts of social exclusion consciously create inequality, based on his theory of social closure (Murphy, 1988), which is derived from Max Weber's (1958) closure theory, in which "formal or informal, overt or covert rules governing the practices of monopolization and exclusion" (p. 1). In my discussion of the City Beautiful movement, I examine social exclusion, following Anne Witz (1992), who uses Murphy's theory to dispute histories that show Gilded Age professionalism as an elite sphere for male administrators who stand apart from so-called semiprofessional clerical workers and field practitioners. Witz (1992) reveals the inequities and power struggles between male and female professionals when she analyzes the pull and haul within social hierarchies of "male and female professional projects" (p. 1). The clubwomen participated in these kinds of professional projects with pubic school teachers (the so-called semiprofessionals) to counter the policies and social attitudes of male administrators.

Chicago public school teachers and CWC clubwomen worked together as a formidable, almost completely female force, with 98% of public school teachers being women (Flanagan, 2002). Conditions are similar today, with the "public school teaching force . . . made up of 76 percent women" (National Education Association, 2010, para. 25) and the General Federation of Women's Clubs (2010) still "support[ing] the arts, preserve natural resources, advance education, [and] encourage civic involvement" (para. 3). CWC clubwomen helped teachers work with increased agency using progressive, student-centered modes of education, which also fought against the CBE's efforts to micromanage teaching from the top down with scientific standards. CWC clubwomen were effective because they had observed the public affairs practiced mostly by men and, thus, learned how to negotiate politics and business. Additional influence came from women who bridged the two worlds of clubwomen and professional work, like the first woman superintendent of Chicago Public Schools, Ella Flagg Young (Wrigley, 1982).

One of the ways the CWC clubwomen and public school teachers troubled the CBE's scientific management (also known as "social efficiency") (Krug, 1964; Wrigley, 1982) was to plunge into debates over "special studies," liberal arts that included art education. Constituents across Chicago's social classes supported the special studies in public schools. As Amburgy (2002) writes, "Progressive educators argued that special studies made schooling more enjoyable. Working men and women saw special studies as means of social empowerment" (p. 109). Despite this public enthusiasm over special studies, however, the CBE wrote them off as "fads and frills." CBE officials argued that all art forms should have a practical and vocational orientation, a perspective that fit their mission to establish industrial arts, not fine arts, as the standard in their vocational schools. In opposition, the CWC's PSAS provided fine arts—murals, art reproductions, and sculpture—in vocational public schools such as Wendell Phillips High School (WPHS).

The PSAS commissions contributed something unique to schools that were, as schools are now, usually governed by scientifically controlled standards (Cohen, 2002; Croly, 1889; Krug, 1964). Art educators like Henry Turner Bailey (1914) saw school decoration as a way to uplift working-class students, not to pigeonhole them with scientific measurement as "dull-minded" working-class students on whom fine arts would be wasted (Gould, 1996, p. 191). He stated, "Beauty, like morals and rationality, must be made the daily and ubiquitous habit of school life" (Bailey, 1914, p. xi).

CWC's local efforts at school decoration were also part of a broader cultural shift from an American culture of words to one of images (Susman, 1984). Just as the World Wide Web brought new ways to distribute text and multimedia in the 21st century, publishers and filmmakers of the early 20th century used new technologies for the mass publication of imagery, which appealed directly to emotions in ways that words did not (Lippmann, 1922). Painter Edward H. Blashfield (1913) knew this; as he told an audience in 1912 at the Art Institute of Chicago, murals were "public and municipal educator[s]" and were didactic more than decorative (p. 8). Following this cultural trend, the most "progressive" school building designs included exhibition and museum spaces for visual education. Though earlier murals existed in Chicago Public School buildings, the earliest CWC commission was at William McKinley High School. The CWC Art and Literature Department appointed Frederic Clay Bartlett to decorate the whole Assembly Hall, including five mural panels that complemented a stained-glass window from a previous commission (Rhor, 2004). After the McKinley murals were finished in 1905, the CWC founded its Public School Art Society (PSAS), which commissioned other murals, not the least of them for Wendell Phillips High School (WPHS).

THE WENDELL PHILLIPS HIGH SCHOOL NEIGHBORHOODS

The first mural commissioned by the PSAS, in 1905, encompassed four panels in the main foyer of Wendell Phillips High School (WPHS). The WPHS murals were as significant to the school as they were to the school's surrounding community. As a racially integrated vocational boys' high school, WPHS, ironically, marked the racial segregation of its four surrounding Chicago neighborhoods. Two were predominantly middle- and upper-class white, Grand Boulevard and Washington Park Court. The other two were Fuller Park and Douglas, neighborhoods with African American populations that increased from 15,000 to 50,000 between 1890 and 1915. African Americans were segregated in Fuller Park and Douglas at the insistence of white residents and landlords (History of Grand Boulevard, n.d.). A few of the clubwomen challenged the racial segregation with their rumblings of intrusion right into the neighborhood. The history of Grand Boulevard identifies Violet Phipps of Washington Park Court as one of the first individuals to rent apartments to African Americans in a predominantly white neighborhood. Phipps would have been considered a "new" or "radical" clubwoman, whose example other women eventually followed (History of Grand Boulevard, n.d.).

Another CWC clubwoman who facilitated efforts on the amelioration of racial tensions along Grand Boulevard was a former president of the Chicago

Woman's Club, Celia Parker Woolley, who was also president and founder of the National Association for the Advancement of Colored People (NA ACP). Woolley also founded the Frederick Douglass Center, in 1904, near WPHS, which provided a place for exchange among middle-class white and African American women on issues that ranged from housing discrimination to suffrage. Even with such worthy intentions, however, contradiction emerged: Woolley felt that African American women "[lacked] the executive ability and [were] incapable of leading" reform movements or serving as president (History of Grand Boulevard, n.d.). So even as the CWC clubwomen made gestures of inclusiveness, they still expressed their own social exclusion. This points to the powerful Anglo-American hegemony that complicated and drove both activists and public officials and signifies how pervasive the context of racism was at that time.

While the CWC clubwomen were instrumental in Chicago's urban reform, they were, at the same time, buried in their Anglo-Protestant middle- and upper-class mentality. Their efforts pushed against the CBE's scientific management and race bias of vocational education (Krug, 1964; Rhor, 2004). All said, in a neighborhood where students were sorted by ethnicity and race, the CWC clubwomen cracked the code of segregation by bringing races together. The WPHS murals signify these conflicts by addressing racial issues, but with contradictions.

WENDELL PHILLIPS HIGH SCHOOL MURALS

The four artists who painted the WPHS murals were Dudley Crafts Watson, of the School of the Art Institute faculty; Lauros Monroe Phoenix from the Federal School in Minneapolis, Minnesota; Gayle Porter Hoskins, Art Institute alumnus and mural designer for Marshall Fields Department Store; and Art Institute alumnus Albert F. Giddings. The subject matter of the mural cycle is historical, reflecting what was perceived as civilization at the time, and reflecting on social attitudes in the immediate neighborhoods and the city. Two murals along the left wall depict Native Americans and European missionaries; those along the right wall, European classical subject matter. The two Native American images depict Native Americans as what social scientists of the time considered "savage." Phoenix's panel shows the European Father Jacques Marquette with Illinois Indians, and Watson's panel shows a Native American family living in an indigenous landscape. On the right are images derived from ancient European civilization. Hoskins's classical figures are draped in togas and robes; and Giddings's draped characters kneel before a seated figure (Rhor, 2004). Juxtaposed this way, the two pairs of murals reflect a popularized view of the frontier of American Westward Expansion as the cultural line between savagery and civilization, as articulated by Frederick Jackson Turner (1893), whose address at the World's Columbian Exhibition in 1893 was positioned to announce the closing of the Western Frontier.

These murals could have been read as a commemoration of the Western Frontier and Westward Expansion, but with ironic connotations related to stereotypes of civilization and savagery.

Given that WPHS was one of the few racially integrated schools at that time, and that all students were male, it is plausible to read the narrative of Marquette and the Illinois Indians as amelioration between races. The narrative could also be read as the suffusion of European culture among Native Americans. On balance, however, other developments at the time the mural was painted were exclusionary and undercut the validity of the peace between races that the murals depicted. Viewers would have been aware of the popular Wild West shows from vaudeville that reenacted fictive "cowboy and Indian" combat as entertainment, and that stereotyped North American Indians as wild and violent. One of these shows, for example, was staged for an audience of 18,000 fairgoers at the World's Columbian Exposition in Chicago in 1893. Impresarios recruited North American Indians for these productions from their reservations who were casted to act as scapegoats for violence on the Western frontier (Reddin, 1999). The WPHS murals thus signified racist narratives that emerged in American popular culture, which also complicated the humane efforts of the PSAS.

BRINGING ART INTO THE SCHOOL

The lesson for contemporary educators and community activists is that community work is still important, and it remains vital to life in American cities. The educational activism of the CWC affected education in their own time, and their work also bears considerations for today's public schooling as well. In the Gilded Age, when the CWC put artworks in vocational school buildings, they created what might be considered informal extensions of the far-removed Art Institute of Chicago into the community life around the school premises. Were it not for the CWC clubwomen's efforts at school beautification, vocational students, who were mostly working-class European immigrants and African Americans, would have been excluded from the fine arts to which genteel audiences had access. The CWC commissions also countered CBE race-biased vocational education policies with their choice of artists. PSAS mural projects sometimes went to professional painters, but commissions like the one for Lane Technical High School went to faculty, alumni, and students of the School of the Art Institute of Chicago (SAIC), among which were women and African American painters (Rhor, 2004). Traditional practice among mural artists in Chicago at that time was to paint a mural in the studio and then take it to the site for installation, but when women painted murals, they worked on location in a more collaborative mode that predated the collaborative models of studio education practiced in the 1970s by artists like Judy Chicago. Their approach to mural painting is another way that women artists, some of whom were CWC clubwomen, broke with the professional practice of mostly male mural artists (Rhor, 2004). In these cases mural painting was done on location in the school building, whereas. In these various ways, the CWC actually reformed art education at the professional level, used the collaborative approach to create assets of visual art for working-class communities, and disrupted Chicago's educational politics (Rhor, 2004).

The CWC's activism bears considerations for today's schools. Back when the CWC provided art education for WPHS and other vocational high schools, they troubled the CBE's paradigm of scientific management with its class and race bias. School administrators commonly sorted higher-achieving students toward academic (liberal arts) programs, and lower-achieving students to vocational programs (with less liberal arts), all based on social Darwinism, itself based on ethnicity and race (Krug, 1964; Spring, 2004). At the end of the 20th century, this tracking still occurred, but school systems privileged science instead of liberal arts. In 1992, a RAND study (Oakes, Selvin, Karoly, & Guiton, 1992) reported that low-income and disadvantaged minority students took more vocational courses than advanced science. The study also reported that vocational students believed that vocational education, not advanced science, was best suited for them, and they therefore saw themselves as unlikely to succeed in advanced science. In this way, expectations set the tone for social exclusion from academic tracks, and race was also an issue. The National Center for Education Statistics (1997) reported that students in advanced science courses were mostly white or Asian, with far fewer African American and American Indian students. As shown in the RAND study, this racial gap reflects how African American and American Indian students were not expected to succeed in, and thus were excluded from, advanced science (Oakes et al., 1992). As these statistics indicate, it would seem that social exclusion by race in recent times has not gone away.

IMPLICATIONS FOR TODAY

As argued at the beginning of this chapter, women's organizations were essential to urban reform in the City Beautiful Movement, and they operated with their own agency to bring about change in Chicago. The CWC clubwomen along with teachers pushed against vocational education policies with the refinement of school decoration; they also negotiated uneasy, complex cultural hierarchies. On one hand, the hegemony of Anglo-American culture and privilege was all-pervasive; school decoration was noble in its intention to improve school life. On the other hand, one cannot ignore that the decorations came from elite European art forms, not the plebeian art forms of working-class European immigrants or of the African Americans who lived in the neighborhoods around WPHS. Indeed, Violet Phipps and Celia Parker Woolley are examples of individuals who recognized culture in their neighborhoods. Going against precedents of racial segregation, they facilitated interracial understanding and made themselves assets for social change. Ironically, however, they also compromised their own good deeds when they limited the opportunities for African American women and denied them leadership positions in women's clubs. Thus emerged an ongoing negotiation between cultural hegemony and efforts toward change.

As clubwomen still do today, in the early 20th century they held the longest influence in the community efforts like the City Beautiful movement. The Chicago Plan as adopted in 1909 was only a small part of this history, and was preempted in 1912 with the head architect Daniel Burnham's untimely death and the death of many other City Beautiful supporters who, ironically, perished on the *Titanic*—itself a floating imperial city—in the North Atlantic Ocean (Manieri-Elia, 1980). In contrast, one can trace the CWC clubwomen's sponsorship of mural work from before the Chicago Plan through the 1920s, and even into the Great Depression (Rhor, 2004).

In the 21st century, the tradition of community work with schools at the street level continues in agencies like parent-teacher organizations, which started as "mothers' associations" in the Gilded Age, and remain an important connection for parents who are asked to become directly involved in the education of their children (Krug, 1964). Yet things also get complicated when, after almost 100 years of reform, scholars still identify deficits when, for example, parents are positioned as subjects and objects of social problems—are blamed for the difficulties of educating children in urban schools, which jeopardizes trust between schools and community (Fine, 1993). In contrast, other associations, like San Francisco's Sunset Neighborhood Beacon Center, identify assets that strengthen school–community relationships by connecting neighborhood assets—families with schools—through after-school programs, a public library, and classes in visual art instruction and electronic media to bring individuals together and position the school as a community social center (Sunset Neighborhood Beacon Center, 2010). Now, as did the CWC, community workers today also use assets at the street level to build stronger neighborhood life, and the tradition of community life is sustained. As did the CWC clubwomen, today's community workers and teachers also foment agency for communities and set examples when they knuckle down and negotiate the justifiably complicated social and racial webs of educational politics and city growth to advocate for neighborhood communities to build themselves strong.

REFERENCES

Amburgy, P. M. (2002). Fads, frills, and basic subjects: Special studies and social conflict in Chicago in 1893. *Studies in Art Education, 43*(2), 109–123.

Bailey, H. T. (1914). *Art education.* Boston, MA: Houghton Mifflin.

Blashfield, E. H. (1913). *Mural painting in America.* New York: Scribners.

Cohen, M. (2002). Art to educate: A history of public art in the New York City public schools, 1890–1976 (Ph.D. dissertation, City University of New York, 2002). Dissertations & Theses: A&I. (Publication No. AAT 3047205)

Condit, C. W. (1973). *Chicago, 1910–1929: Building, planning, and urban technology.* Chicago: University of Chicago Press.

Croly, J. C. (1898). *The history of the woman's club movement in America.* New York: Henry & Allen & Company.

Fine, M. (1993). [Ap]parent involvement: Reflections on parents, power, and urban public schools. & Responses. *Teachers College Record, 94*(4), 1–19. Retrieved from http://www.tcrecord.org/content.asp?contentid=147.

Flanagan, M. (2002). *Seeing with their hearts: Chicago women and the vision of the good city, 1871–1933.* Princeton, NJ: Princeton University Press.

General Federation of Women's Clubs. (2010). *About GFWC.* Retrieved from http://www.gfwc.org/gfwc/About_GFWC.asp?SnID=1995583784.

Gould, S. J. (1996). *The mismeasure of man.* New York: Norton.

History of Grand Boulevard, Volume 1, Part 1. Vivien Palmer Oral Histories of Chicago Neighborhoods, the Chicago Historical Society, boxes 1–6.

Krug, E. A. (1964). *The shaping of the American high school.* New York: Harper & Row.

Lippmann, W. (1922). *Public opinion.* New York: Free Press.

Manieri-Elia, M. (1980). Toward an "imperial city": Daniel H. Burnham and the City Beautiful movement. In G. Ciucci, F. Dal Co, M. Manieri-Elia, & M. Tafuri (Eds.), *The American city* (pp. 8–19). London: Granada.

Murphy, R. (1988). *Social closure: The theory of monopolization and exclusion.* Oxford: Clarendon Press.

National Center for Educational Statistics. (1997). *Science proficiency and course taking in high school.* Retrieved from http://nces.ed.gov/pubs97/97838.asp.

National Education Association. (2010). *Best gift for teachers on National Teacher Day? Their jobs. Five trends—including massive layoffs—provide portrait of nation's public school teachers.* Retrieved from http://www.nea.org/home/39198.htm.

Oakes, J., Selvin, M., Karoly, S. A., & Guiton, G. (1992). *Educational matchmaking: Academic and vocational tracking in comprehensive high schools.* Santa Monica, CA: Rand Corporation.

Reddin, P. (1999). *Wild West shows.* Champaign-Urbana, IL: University of Illinois Press.

Rhor, S. C. (2004). *Mural painting and public schools in Chicago, 1905–1941* (Ph.D. dissertation, University of Pittsburgh, 2004). Dissertations & Theses: A&I. (Publication No. AAT 3139714)

Schlereth, T. J. (1992). *Cultural history and material culture: Everyday life, landscapes museums.* Charlottesville, VA: University Press of Virginia.

Spring, J. (2004). *The American school, 1642–2004.* Boston: McGraw-Hill.

Sunset Neighborhood Beacon Center. (2010). *Sunset Neighborhood Beacon Center: A safe place for youth and families to learn and grow.* San Francisco, CA: Sunset Neighborhood Beacon Center. Retrieved from http://snbc.org/about/history

Susman, W. I. (1984). *Culture as history: The transformation of American society in the twentieth century.* New York: Pantheon Books.

Szczygiel, B. (2003). "City beautiful" revisited: An analysis of nineteenth-century civic improvement efforts. *Journal of Urban History, 29*(2), 107–132.

Turner, F. J. (1893). *The significance of the frontier in American history*. American Historical Association, Chicago, July 12, 1893.

Weber, M. (1958). *Max Weber: Essays in sociology*. New York: Oxford University Press.

Wilson, W. H. (1989). *The City Beautiful movement*. Baltimore, MD: Johns Hopkins University Press.

Witz, A. (1992). *Professions and patriarchy*. London: Routledge.

Wrigley, J. (1982). *Class politics and public schools: Chicago, 1900–1950*. New Bruswick, NJ: Rutgers University Press.

Counternarratives

Considering Urban Students' Voices in Art Education

JESSIE L. WHITEHEAD

> Students burst into classrooms with energy and desire and intention. Each
> brings a voice, a set of experiences and knowledge and know-how, a way
> of seeing and thinking and being. Each, again, is an unruly spark of
> meaning-making energy on a voyage of discovery.
> —William Ayers, *Teaching Toward Freedom*

In large cities such as Chicago, Los Angeles, New York, and Washington, DC, half
or more of these energetic public school students are students of color (Lewis &
Moore, 2008). I currently reside in Connecticut, and this percentage is specifically reflected in New Haven public schools where student demographics consist
of 1.24% Asian Americans, 54.82% African Americans, 30.95% Hispanics, 0.05%
Native Americans, 11.08% Whites, and 1.86% Other (http://www.nhps.net/
nhpsdemographics). According to Garcia (2002), the urban student population
comes from families that are linguistically, culturally, socially, economically, and
religiously different. This population includes recent immigrants as well as African American, Native American, and European American students whose families
have lived in the United States for generations. Garcia (2002) suggests that these
diverse students are noticed only after they are labeled as limited English proficient, poor, low-performing, immigrant, and so on and consequently segregated
and ostracized in schools that still cater to "mainstream" Americans through both
culturally and socially inadequate pedagogy and curricular content.

Urban students' visibility must not be associated with these demeaning clas-
sifications. We need to more clearly *see* urban students by recognizing their humanity and their potential as complex individuals. As Ayers (2004) asserts in the
opening quote to this chapter, urban students enter classrooms with *knowledge*,
information, and *experiences*. Through a commitment to ensure the visibility of
each student as a person, educators can contribute to a radical reversal, in which
"the student becomes a source of knowledge and information and energy, actor,

speaker, creator, constructor, thinker, doer—a teacher as well as a learner" (p. 42). The majority of these urban students who are systematically discounted by schools are individuals of color and, as Bernal (2002) reminds us, possessors and creators of knowledge, who often feel as if "their histories, experiences, cultures, languages are devalued, misinterpreted, or omitted within formal educational settings" (p. 106).

As a person of color and a teacher, I have firsthand experience with this state of invisibility. I have been subject to it at times in my own schooling and tried my best not to reproduce it in my practice as an art educator. As an art teacher, I see all my students as creators, constructors, thinkers, and doers. From working with students in the past and in my capacity as a teacher educator in a university setting, I have articulated my belief that the field of art education can play a significant role in transforming urban education. Art education experiences can provide significant opportunities for students to articulate, represent, and imagine their histories, experiences, and cultures in richer and more in-depth ways. Recognizing students as sources of knowledge and information encourages teachers to also utilize their students as a primary asset to their own educations and to the schools they attend.

In this chapter, I propose that we look beyond labels and more readily consider the voices of urban students in terms of the value they bring to education in general and art education in particular. I suggest we model this process of recognition on the work of contemporary artists of color who use forms of *counternarrative* (Desai, 2010) with the goal of challenging established and often limited views with more inclusive and socially just ones. An art and education approach based on the notion of *counterstorytelling* can provide ways to bring out the voices of students as important, readily available assets to education. Counterstorytelling is a strategy drawn from critical race theory (Delgado & Stefancic, 2001) to address the damaging effects of racism as experienced in the United States. To combat institutional racism[1] such as it is experienced in many urban schools, critical race theory scholars maintain that it is essential for marginalized students to tell their ways of understanding and experiencing the world. These emerging voices simultaneously challenge the educational status quo and announce possibilities for urban education (Barton & O'Neill, 2008).

This chapter aims to construct a vision of how counterstorytelling can offer truly transformative opportunities for urban art education by building on an understanding of students as assets and reflecting practices of contemporary artists. I focus on urban students of color because as Bernal (2002) states, although they comprise the majority population in urban schools, often their histories, experiences, and perspectives are devalued, misinterpreted, or omitted. My identity as a Black American and a teacher also strongly plays a part in my passion to engage in and promote socially transformative educational practices that honor and recognize difference and heterogeneity as an asset. Additionally, Desai (2010) reminds us that when we systematically ignore or silence the voices of students of color, we normalize whiteness and contribute to the new social malaise of color-blind racism.

COUNTERSTORYTELLING AND CRITICAL RACE THEORY

Critical race theory began around the mid-1970s. Lawyers, activists, and legal scholars in the United States were concerned that the advances of the civil rights era of the 1960s were eroding and new theories and strategies were needed to combat racism (Delgado & Stefancic, 2001). The theory is no longer solely confined to the law but has expanded into other fields, including education. Solórzano and Yosso (2002) point out that applications of critical race theory in education (1) focus on how students of color experience and respond to the United States educational system and (2) challenge the pervasiveness of cultural deficit stories through approaches such as counterstorytelling, oral traditions, historiographies, poetry, and films. Seeking to restore authentic and empowering understandings of self and complex understandings of surrounding conditions, the commonality among these approaches is the reliance on shared stories.

This chapter examines the potential of counterstorytelling for urban education. Solórzano and Yosso (2002) define *counterstory* as "a method of telling the stories of those people whose experiences are not often told (i.e., those on the margins of society)" (p. 32). Counterstorytelling is an approach that can help bring out the individual voices, sets of experiences, and ways of seeing, thinking, and being (Ayers, 2004) of a student population often placed at the margins of schooling. Revealing the complexity of experiences in the urban setting of the Bronx (New York), Asher's (2000) vivid account emphasizes the importance of art education to provide an avenue for urban students to share their perspectives—positive perspectives that can counter the negative imagery often associated with urban settings:

> Their own stories became important information and resources for transforming personal images into art. My students lived where crime, unswept streets, and empty crack vials are common. It is difficult for people to see beyond this pervasive reality, yet some do, and such a program can help to integrate those images into another more positive perspective. Within this squalor there are views that reflect the hope of people struggling to create a productive life. Schools and other learning institutions can help provide options for these young people to accomplish this. (p. 38)

Bell (2010) identifies *concealed, resistance,* and *emerging/transforming* stories as the three categories of counterstories that challenge *stock* stories, which are narratives told by the dominant group. Stock stories are public and ever-present in mainstream institutions of society, such as schools. They reveal what society considers important and meaningful, and support the status quo (Bell, 2010). In classrooms stock stories are pervasive and evident in the contents of curricula, textbooks, and teachers' discourses that continue to predominantly reflect Eurocentric history, values, and culture. Stock stories also include urban tales that students of color hear about themselves in which they are continuously labeled as at risk and low achievers.

In the area of art education, stock stories relate to artists of the Western canon, the icons, the *canned artists* who have a long shelf life and who have been deemed important and universally meaningful to students. For decades, students have been continuously taught about O'Keefe, Picasso, van Gogh, and other European or Euro-American artists. Classroom walls are proudly adorned with reproductions of these artists' work. There are also look-alikes by students. Students' learning experiences are dominated by overexposure to these artists. The stock art curriculum usually lacks information about artists of color and artistic movements associated with them. If they enter the curriculum at all, African American artists such as Jacob Lawrence, Romare Bearden, and Alma Thomas are often limited to Black History Month (the shortest month of the year), representing a type of concealment.

Concealed stories often remain hidden from mainstream view, pushed into the margins. Once told, they reveal hidden stories from the perspective of people marginalized and often stigmatized by the dominant society, as well as stories that illustrate how race shapes experience. *Resistance stories* teach about antiracist perspectives and practices and serve as inspiration and the foundation for continued fashioning of new stories. *Emerging/transforming stories* build on concealed and resistance stories; they constitute new stories that advance antiracism and social justice work, engaging contemporary action against racism. Several contemporary artists create art that functions as a form of counternarrative. These artists' practices seek to reveal hidden stories, develop resistance strategies, and provide new stories.

CONTEMPORARY COUNTERSTORYTELLERS

Contemporary counterstorytellers such as artists Kerry James Marshall, Charlene Teters, Vincent Valdez, and Fred Wilson use their voices to challenge stock stories. For example, Marshall creates visual narratives about the political and social invisibility of Blacks (Whitehead, 2009), as well as the Black American urban experience. "The Lost Boys" series relates to Black American youth's lost innocence, youth in the inner city who are deprived of the opportunity to grow up because of the loss of lives at an early age due to violence, and loss of innocence as a result of imprisonment (Marshall, 2000). Teters uses her artwork to counter the inappropriate use of the "history of Native people, their culture, and icons in images that was deflating to my children and me" (Whitehead, 2008, p. 31). Her work reveals the hidden racism associated with the use of Native Americans as mascots, and provides a lens to look at the racism connected to the historical and current experiences of Native peoples.

Valdez and Wilson also use visual narratives as counterstories to address the challenges of being a minority in United States. Wilson created a series of museum installations called *Mining the Museum* to illustrate how museums potentially reinforce racist beliefs and behavior. For example, in one such installation called *Cabinetmaking, 1820–1960*, Wilson juxtaposed a group of high-end wooden chairs with a whipping post used for beating slaves. According to Thelma Golden, chief curator of the Studio Museum in Harlem, "*Mining the Museum* changed the way I understood what it meant to put objects in a public space" (quoted in Hoban, 2003, http://nymag.com/nymetro/arts/features/n_9014/).

Vincent Valdez worked for 2 years on a large-scale oil painting created on the surface of a 1953 Chevy ice-cream truck. The narrative work tells a decade of history of El Chavez Ravine, a Mexican-American working class neighborhood in Los Angeles that was indiscriminately destroyed to make room for the Dodgers stadium. The chronological account is rich with symbolism that captures the Mexican-American experience as disposable members of society with limited social capital. Images include ghost-like images of residents, the faces of the puppet masters of this gentrification effort, and icons of the American experience—bald eagles, flags, the Chevrolet insignia. As we walk around the ice-cream truck, itself a symbol of cultural assimilation—in many instances the only outside vehicle to penetrate certain ethnic neighborhoods, we witness the process of displacement of this community. This violent transformation that in many cases involved forceful police removal of families, is almost forgotten today. The work's final scene is depicted from the vantage point of the stands of Dodgers ball game. We are invited to be cheerful spectators and join the many Mexican American patrons who ignore or are unfamiliar with the history that took place there.

The visual narratives of these four artists represent a deliberate form of counterstorytelling, highlighting one of the purposes of counterstories, which is to build a community among those at the margins of society (Solórzano & Yosso, 2002). The artists' works and their content reflect experiences of those outside of dominant culture. These artists' practices of using visual narratives to articulate voice and meaning of their life experiences and to respond to their environment can inspire educational approaches that facilitate urban students' use of counternarratives as a means to give voice to their stories.

COUNTERSTORYTELLING AND URBAN ART EDUCATION

Implementing the counterstorytelling approaches in urban education can impact the experience of urban students by bringing a heightened visibility to them.

Countering the negative stories often portrayed by the media, students' stories can open up avenues to express the pride they have in themselves and their communities. These self-generated narratives also provide a way to share challenges students face at school and in their lives. Viewing and listening to these stories places us in the role of the learner, and provides an opportunity to better understand our students. These counterstories/images reinstate students' identities and have the potential to build a community within classrooms as a result of shared narratives.

Urban art education benefits from a heightened student visibility because each student voice contributes to transforming and enhancing curricula. In art, the articulation of students' voices through counterstories unveils to each student the process of creating and interpreting meaning. Students' racialized experiences must inform educational planning and shift the curriculum focus beyond the European American experience, particularly in art. This transformational approach reveals to diverse urban students that they matter and are recognized and appreciated in their own environment (Lindsey, Karns, & Myatt, 2010).

Counterstorytelling can be an agent of expression that has the potential for altering urban art education by (1) developing stronger student voices throughout the educational experience; (2) challenging the status quo as traditionally presented in curricular materials, art and other subject textbooks, and mainstream discourses that continue to predominantly reflect Eurocentric history, values, and culture; and (3) encouraging educators to provide alternatives to stock stories that are not necessarily relevant to today's urban students. It is important for educators to understand and value the culture of students and their communities, which consists of people with assets to be recognized and valued by schools (Lindsey, Karns, & Myatt, 2010).

URBAN STUDENTS AS ASSETS

The art education I propose addresses the goals of understanding and valuing the culture of students and their communities through (1) acknowledging the wealth of resources contained in urban environments relevant to learning and teaching about visual art; (2) drawing upon the creative and cultural assets of the urban community to direct community-building through art; (3) creating opportunities for more meaningful art educational experiences; and (4) transforming the way we view urban students.

Lindsey, Karns, and Myatt (2010) argue that educators are too often constrained by thinking and practice that view students by "who they are not" or "what they don't have" rather than "what it is they bring to school on which we can build" (p. 18). Acknowledging students' strengths helps them feel that they can contribute to their educational growth (Paek, 2008). There are examples of this asset-based approach, such as the community art program conducted by Hutzel

(2007), which illustrates students contributing to their own educational growth. The program took place in a primarily low-income African American neighborhood in Cincinnati known as the West End. The students' participation in the community art project provided opportunities for them to share their perceptions of the West End neighborhood. Their participation involved creating drawings of their concept of community, constructing asset-based maps that pinpointed good things about their neighborhood, and allowing themselves to be interviewed. The students' contributions factored in the creation of two neighborhood murals, and as Hutzel (2007) states, "Their opinions, ideas, and perceptions were central to the development of the art pieces" (p. 307). Examples in other disciplines including math (Paek, 2008) and science (Barton & O'Neill, 2008)[2] reveal the potential of the use of students as assets. The simple realization that urban students are the key to engendering meaningful art and education practices can direct positive transformations in urban schools.

BUILDING ON STUDENTS' STRENGTHS

As stated at the beginning, this chapter is an attempt to construct a vision of how counterstorytelling can offer transformative opportunities for urban art education that build on students' assets and reflect the practices of contemporary artists. As Kretzmann and McKnight (1993) inform us, an asset-based viewpoint promotes focusing on strengths and making use of available resources present in the urban community that can be used to achieve positive change. Smith-Maddox and Solórzano (2002) remind us that counterstorytelling focuses on including the narrative of those outside the dominant culture. Combining these notions, this chapter suggests that art education experiences can provide a powerful way to engage students in a different kind of urban education practice.

The majority of students in the urban environment are children of color who are mainly viewed as outside the dominant culture. These diverse students are often noticed only by their perceived deficiencies (Garcia, 2002), which basically render the students invisible as individuals. It is important that we stop seeing these students as labels but as unique individuals with important stories to tell. Through the use of counterstorytelling, urban art education has the opportunity to construct a teaching and learning climate that more overtly includes the narratives of the students, recognizing the wealth of knowledge and experiences they bring into classrooms. In doing so, we show students that they matter, and that we respect their richness and encourage their creativity and gifts.

Imagine walking into a classroom where compelling contemporary works by artists of color are displayed and used as inspiration year-round, expanding the canon of European and Euro-American artists. Modeling the practices of contemporary artists, students can share their personal experiences, knowledge, and responses to being viewed as outside the margins of mainstream culture. Students in this environment are creators, constructors, thinkers, and doers who are encouraged and supported to take advantage of the unique opportunities art provides to narrate their stories. Many stories have been told through art, in urban schools art education is an important avenue to articulate students' voices. Honoring each student's perspective, art education practices are essential to urban school transformation, allowing students to articulate their counterstories, engage in dialogue with dominant stories, and participate in the transformation of their lives.

NOTES

1. Institutional racism is a complex, multifaceted concept. Some definitions, for example, focus on the outcome of segregation and inequality, while others focus on the outcome of unearned privileges and advantages. Frequently, definitions stress that once racism takes hold and is embedded within institutions it does not require "intent." Rather, institutional racism can be perpetuated by seemingly benign policies, practices, behaviors, traditions, structures, and so on, which is why it usually goes unchallenged (http://www.eraseracismny.org/html/whatis/whatis.php).

2. This article does not specifically address counterstorytelling, but the students' roles are a good example of assets.

REFERENCES

Asher, R. (2000). The Bronx as art: Exploring the urban environment. *Art Education, 53*(4), 33–38.

Ayers, W. (2004). *Teaching toward freedom: Moral commitment and ethical action in the classroom.* Boston, MA: Beacon Press.

Bailey, C., & Desai, D. (2005). Visual art and education: Engaged visions of history and community. *Multicultural Perspectives, 7*(1), 39–43.

Barton, A. C., & O'Neill, T. (2008). Counter-storytelling in science: Authoring a place in the worlds of science and community. In R. Levinson, H. Nicholson, & S. Parry (Eds.), *Creative encounters: New conversations in science education and the arts* (pp. 138–158). London: Wellcome Trust.

Bell, L. A. (2010). *Storytelling for social justice: Connecting narrative and the arts in antiracist teaching.* New York: Routledge.

Bernal, D. (2002). Critical race theory, Latcrit theory, and critical-raced gendered epistemologies: Recognizing students of color as holders and creators of knowledge. *Qualitative Inquiry, 8*(1), 105–126.

Delgado, R., & Stefancic, J. (2001). *Critical race theory: An introduction.* New York: NYU Press.

Desai, D. (2010). The challenge of new colorblind racism in art education. *Art Education, 63*(2), 22–28.

Garcia, E. (2002). Foreword. In D. F. Brown, *Becoming a successful urban teacher*. Portsmouth, NH: Heinemann.

Hoban, P. (2003, July). The shock of the familiar. New York Magazine.com. Retrieved from http://nymag.com/nymetro/arts/features/n_9014/.

Hutzel, K. (2007). Reconstructing a community, reclaiming a playground: A participatory action research study. *Studies in Art Education, 48*(3), 299–315.

Kailin, J. (2002). *Anti-racist education: From theory to practice*. Lanham, MD: Rowman & Littlefield.

Kretzmann, J. P., & McKnight, J. L. (1993). *Building communities from the inside out: A path toward finding and mobilizing a community's assets*. Evanston, IL: Institute for Policy Research, Northwestern University.

Lewis, C. W., & Moore, J. L. (2008). Urban public schools for African American students: Critical issues for educational stakeholders. *Journal of Educational Foundations, 22*(1–3), 3–10.

Lindsey, R. B., Karns, M. S., & Myatt, K. (2010). *Culturally proficient education: An asset-based response to conditions of poverty*. Thousand Oaks, CA: Corwin.

Marshall, K. (2000). *Kerry James Marshall*. New York: Harry N. Abrams.

Paek, P. L. (2008, January). Building teacher capacity. Cross-case analysis from practices worthy of attention: Local innovations in strengthening secondary mathematics. Unpublished manuscript. Austin: Charles A. Dana Center at The University of Texas at Austin. Retrieved from http://www.utdanacenter.org/pwoa/downloads/pwoa_teacher_capacity.pdf

Smith-Maddox, R., & Solórzano, D. G. (2002). Using critical race theory, Paulo Freire's problem-posing method, and case study research to confront race and racism in education. *Qualitative Inquiry, 8*(1), 66–84.

Solórzano, D. G., & Yosso, T. J. (2002). Critical race methodology: Counter-storytelling as an analytical framework for education research. *Qualitative Inquiry, 8*(1), 23–44.

Whitehead, J. L. (2008). Theorizing experience: Four women of color. *Studies in Art Education, 50*(1), 22–35.

Whitehead, J. L. (2009). Invisibility of blackness. *Art Education, 62*(2), 33–39.

Part II

Reimagining Teacher Education Through Art: The Dialectic of Freedom

KIM COSIER

> My focal interest is . . . in the capacity to surpass the given and look at things as if they could be otherwise.
> —Maxine Greene, *The Dialectic of Freedom*

If a democratic society is to thrive, the education of its children must be a priority. In order to teach our children well, the education of teachers must also be held as a fundamental concern. Support for pre-service and in-service teachers through meaningful educational and professional development opportunities should, therefore, be woven into the very fabric of our society. For teachers and children in urban schools, teacher education issues take on even greater urgency than they do in more affluent, suburban schools. Dropout rates persist at 50% in many city schools, and the achievement gap between children of color and white children remains stubbornly fixed at unacceptable levels (Kailin, 2002).

Research has shown that teachers can have an enormous influence on student success in urban schools (Darling-Hammond & Bransford, 2005; Gordon, Kane, & Staiger, 2006), yet education policy in the United States penalizes teachers in urban schools for taking on the enormous challenges they face every day. There was hope that the Obama administration would make substantive changes in federal education policy; however, as it stands, the federal mandate for "highly qualified teachers" only narrowly conceives of what high qualifications mean (Darling-Hammond & Baratz-Snowden, 2005; Westheimer & suurtamm, 2009). Current policy punishes pupils and school personnel for lagging achievement scores in a narrowly conceived curriculum. Art, while being given lip service in the initial phases of the No Child Left Behind era, has been increasingly edged out of many schools. Because art is not on the tests, it is cut from the curriculum to provide more time for the "core" subjects that do appear on high-stakes tests. Yet we know that art can make a difference in the lives of children and youth, particularly art instruction that is grounded in an ethic of social justice.

An activist stance, in which a teacher sees herself as a change-maker as well as an instructor, has been shown to be the key to success in urban schools (Cochran-Smith, 2004). New and veteran teachers alike need time and support to develop the reflective praxis necessary to become effective educational activists. Social justice can fall by the wayside as educators struggle to keep their heads above water without proper support. The authors in this section recognize the essentially activist nature of urban teacher education for democracy and social justice. They believe it is possible to help pre-service and in-service teachers jump through the many bureaucratic hoops set before them while still tending a passion for the larger purposes of education. In art education, this means connecting teachers to the sense of wonder and possibility about which Maxine Greene (1988) teaches so eloquently, inspiring them to "look at things as if they could be otherwise" (p. 3).

Our contributors offer examples of site-specific yet adaptable approaches to urban art teacher education, highlighting programs that face challenges but focus on possibilities inherent in teaching art in urban settings. I begin the section with a chapter that discusses my theoretical evolution as an urban art teacher educator and outlines the impact of theory on the art education program in Milwaukee, Wisconsin. Leda Guimarães considers the contemporary global city as a "culturally quilted pedagogical space" in which educators engage with aesthetic experiences in the complex and plural world of Goiânia, the capital of Goiás State in Brazil. In her story about how pre-service teachers discovered a compelling historical narrative by researching the urban visualities of the neighborhood in which they will teach, Guimarães calls upon urban art teacher educators to leave the classroom to mine the city for culturally relevant curriculum. Donalyn Heise and Bryna Bobick, who work with pre-service and in-service art teachers in Memphis, Tennessee, discuss a service learning project, the Community Arts Academy, that was based on resilience theory. Their program enacted an asset-based, collaborative, and playful approach to art education in the city. In the final chapter of the section, Olivia Gude and I have a conversation about a community-asset-based approach to urban art teacher preparation that insists on the interdependence of theory and practice. We argue for an approach to urban art education that sees teachers as cultural workers who can derive great benefit from seeing themselves as part of the complex web of the urban community.

REFERENCES

Cochran-Smith, M. (2004). *Walking the road: Race, diversity, and social justice in teacher educa-tion.* New York: Teachers College Press.

Darling-Hammond, L., & Baratz-Snowden, J. (Eds.). (2005). *A good teacher in every classroom: Preparing the highly qualified teachers our children deserve.* National Academy of Educa-tion Committee on Teacher Education. San Francisco, CA: Jossey-Bass.

Darling-Hammond, L., & Bransford, J. (Eds.). (2005). *Preparing teachers for a changing world: The report of the Committee on Teacher Education of the National Academy of Education.* San Francisco, CA: Jossey-Bass.

Gordon, R., Kane, T. J., & Staiger, D. O. (2006). *Identifying effective teachers using performance on the job.* Washington, DC: The Brookings Institution.

Greene, M. (1988). *The dialectic of freedom.* New York: Teachers College Press.

Kailin, J. (2002). *Anti-racist education: From theory to practice.* Lanham, MD: Rowman & Littlefield.

Westheimer, J. & suurtamm, k.e. (2009). The politics of social justice meets practice: Teacher education and school change. In W. Ayers, T. Quinn, & D. Stovall (Eds.), *Handbook of social justice in education* (pp. 589–593). New York: Routledge.

4

My Life in Teaching

On an Evolving Teacher Education Praxis for Social Justice

KIM COSIER

Theory, of course, just means thinking about things, puzzling over what is going on, and reflecting on the process of that puzzling and thinking.

—Griselda Pollock, *Conceptual Odysseys*

Teaching is demanding and complex, and teaching art in an urban school can be overwhelmingly so. Preparing novice teachers for a life in urban art education, therefore, presents tremendous challenges and hard-won rewards. I believe that teacher educators who work in urban schools have a moral imperative to join with novice and seasoned teachers alike to become seekers of truth about themselves, others, and the society in which we live. We must work together to be change agents and champions of justice.

In this chapter, I use my teacher autobiography as a way to sketch the contours of what I believe to be priorities of high-quality urban art teacher education. In particular, I focus on my own process of ongoing critical reflection to discuss what I have come to regard as important theoretical, philosophical, and practical features in the preparation and professional development of teachers of urban children and youth.

Cochran-Smith (2004) describes using personal narratives as a teacher education strategy that brings about meaningful reflection. According to Cochran-Smith (2004), such essays allow "prospective teachers as well as experienced teachers and teacher educators . . . opportunities to examine much of what is usually unexamined in the tightly braided relationships of language, culture and power in schools and schooling" (p. 49). In the following, I share my own teaching autobiography to illustrate the development of my stance toward what matters in the preparation and ongoing education of teachers in urban schools.

"TEACHING WOULD BE GREAT,
IF IT WASN'T FOR THE CHILDREN"

When people learn that I used to be a middle school art teacher, they usually wonder aloud about the sanity of a person who would willingly spend her days with adolescents. In fact, I derived great joy from teaching my middle school students. I still miss being included in the daily lives of young people newly capable of understanding humor (both sophisticated and scatological). I miss watching students, still too young to drive, try on adult roles with childlike enthusiasm, and I miss cajoling grumpy resisters into making something that they could be proud of having made.

The days of smoke-filled teachers' lounges had passed by the time I entered the profession, but the atmosphere in the break room was toxic, nonetheless. "Hey, Cosier! I've got another kid for your kiln!" was a line that greeted me regularly in the teachers' lounge. A chorus of bitter laughter always followed, with others adding to a roll call of names, the usual suspects, students my colleagues would gladly have dropped rather than find a way to teach. Now, it's not that I don't enjoy gallows humor, but this gag started off lame and just became more tedious with time. I eventually stopped eating lunch in the teachers' lounge, finding that dullness and cynicism gave me indigestion. As a result, I ended most days with more hope and energy than I had in the past. This is when a seed was planted for what has become a central theme of my teaching philosophy: *In order to teach for social justice, you must not succumb to cynicism; rather, you must train your eyes to see the possible.*

I invited other staff members to join me for lunch in my art classroom, those who shared a more optimistic outlook on life in school. Eventually we invited some of the usual suspects to eat with us and found that they behaved themselves quite well. Those same students regularly got into trouble in the cafeteria, which I believe was in no small part due to the fact that they had a reputation to uphold. This is when another of the central themes of my teaching philosophy began to develop: *If you treat students like human beings, regardless of reputation or stereotype, they usually live up to your expectations.*

I believed then (and still believe) that I was privileged to work with young people who were beginning to wrestle with the larger questions of life—the questions about which adult cynics too often scoff but whose asking is central to a life fully lived. In fact, it was not the roller-coaster mood swings of adolescence but the negativity and cynicism of too many of my teacher colleagues that prompted me to leave my former life teaching art to middle school students and enter into a life in teacher education. I packed up my art room, said a tearful goodbye to my students and a few teacher comrades, and embarked on a new adventure in graduate school at Indiana University.

DISCOVERING THE LARGER PARTS OF TEACHING

While at IU, I discovered that my undergraduate art teacher preparation program had not attended to the larger purposes of education. My experiences as an undergraduate were not all that different from those of others (Fehr, Fehr, & Kiefer-Boyd, 2000). I learned lesson planning and curriculum development, classroom management strategies, and ways to translate studio practice into developmentally appropriate classroom activities. I was an undergraduate when Discipline-Based Art Education (Dobbs, 1992) was all the rage, so I also learned how to incorporate art history, art criticism, and a smattering of aesthetics into the mix.

Most teacher education programs focus on techniques and strategies rather than the moral purposes of education (Gude, 2000). According to Irvine (quoted in Cochran-Smith, 2004, p. xii), "The field of teacher education has not taken seriously its role to prepare teachers as activists and advocates for social justice." Focusing narrowly on methods rather than ideas, my training had not asked me to think deeply or to ask the big, important questions of teaching, such as, What and who is teaching for? (Ayers, Quinn, & Stovall, 2009).

In graduate school my eyes were opened to the urgency of such questions and ideas. First, I was delighted to find that feminism wasn't dead after all! I was pushed to look at art, subjectivity, and representation through newly focused eyes because of Griselda Pollock's (1992, 1996) feminist interrogations of art history, as well as the ongoing ripple effect of Linda Nochlin's (1971) provocative question, "Why have there been no great women artists?" I also learned that education was not the neutral ground my undergraduate program had supposed it to be as I read bell hooks (1994) and other feminist scholars (Ellsworth, 1989; Lather, 1998).

Feminist theory is infused throughout the work of my mentor, Dr. Enid Zimmerman (Cosier, 2010; Zimmerman, 1998). Other notable art educators wrestled with the educational and epistemological implications of feminism, including Elizabeth Garber (1996) and Georgia Collins and Renee Sandell (1984, 1996). Yvonne Gaudelius (2000) connected feminism to critical pedagogy:

> Both feminist and critical pedagogies position teaching as cultural practice. Both approaches consider the impact of formal education on society. . . . Both guide students to examine the processes through which society creates knowledge. Both enable students to contribute to knowledge production. Finally, although these two forms of pedagogy question authority in different ways, empowerment is the goal of both. (p. 23)

Critical pedagogy and the scholarship of the New Left emerged as an intense interest for me. Having grown up a poor, working-class kid, Neo-Marxist analyses of capitalist relations of exploitation in schools and society spoke to me in a very personal way. I discovered the emancipatory promise of critical pedagogy in the work of Paulo Freire (1970), which inspired me as it has so many others, including hooks (1994), Lareau (1989), McLaren (1989), and Giroux (Giroux & McLaren, 1989). I learned to see social relations in schooling through the prism of hegemony (Gramsci, 1971), a powerful analytical tool that seeks to reveal hidden power relationships by asking, "Who benefits?"

Finally, a related area of study concerned the moral implications of teaching. Ayers (2004), Greene (1988), and Noddings (1992) stand out as most influential in this vein, with their challenging but accessible work on moral issues in teaching and the role of imagination and care in education.

In graduate school the profound dialectic that emerged between theory and practice was both exhilarating and challenging. Early on, I chafed at the apparent disconnect between the two, but ultimately I surrendered to the seduction of ideas because they matter. In fact, once I became acclimated to the density of the work of many theorists, I found support to deepen my homegrown ideas: In order to teach for social justice, you must not succumb to cynicism; rather, you must train your eyes to see the possible, and if you treat students like human beings, regardless of reputation or stereotype, they usually live up to your expectations.

My graduate education armed me with the theoretical tools I thought necessary to move on to a position that would allow me to build an art teacher education program focused on teaching for social justice. I believed I was sufficiently educated as I left the nest of graduate school—but that feeling didn't last long.

FINDING MYSELF NEEDING
MORE THEORETICAL GUIDANCE

I took a position at the University of Wisconsin-Milwaukee, where I still find myself happily working today. The decision to come to Milwaukee was not made lightly. I knew that the faculty expected a colleague who would sharpen the program's focus on urban art education. I was excited by the opportunity to work in a place that was committed to social justice, but the urban imperative left me feeling like something of a fraud. After all, I had never worked as a teacher or gone to school in an urban setting. For a couple of years during my childhood I had lived in an "inner-city" homeless shelter but my parents, fearful of their progeny attending city schools, managed to wrangle scholarships for my siblings and me at a private Baptist school. What did I know from urban schools?

In addition to feeling inadequate by way of past experience, I also was apprehensive of taking on what were certain to be insurmountable problems in the urban schools. Like most people without firsthand experience, I was familiar with only the *Savage Inequalities* (Kozol, 1991) of urban classrooms. I was afraid of stepping into a world tipped too far toward injustice—it was a real test of commitment to my first dictum about teaching for social justice through hope rather than cynicism.

I was also afraid that urban children of color would not respond to my efforts to build rapport with them (which had always been one of my strengths as a teacher). What if the young people of the Milwaukee Public Schools did not give me a chance to make connections with them? In truth, I am embarrassed to admit, I was afraid of being rejected by 6-year-olds. Here, then, was a challenge to my second teaching belief about students living up to your expectations when you treat them like human beings, not stereotypes.

I had to ask myself: "Do you, or do you not, mean what you say about wanting to make a difference in the world?"

I did. So I stepped, gingerly at first, into the roiling waters of urban education. It was a lot like walking my dogs in the Milwaukee River—the ground beneath my feet felt rocky and unstable, and I occasionally fell and got soaking wet, but the connection I felt to life was extraordinary and not to be missed!

My students and I began making our first, inelegant steps toward real dialogue about race and social justice. Although our university is located in the city, my students are nearly all white, from suburbs and small towns outside Milwaukee. Like many people from the northern part of the United States, most do not believe that racism is a part of their lives. As I discovered, there can be much resistance to the difficult dialogues that arise when talking about racism from student teachers who consider themselves to be color-blind. As Irvine affirms:

> Some teacher educators and their pre- and in-service teachers discover that discussion of race and ethnicity produce discomfort, guilt, anger, and ultimately denial. Too many of the profession appear to be not only colorblind, but "color deaf" and "color mute" when it comes to issues of race—that is, unable or unwilling to see, hear, or speak about instances of individual or institutional racism in their personal or professional lives. (quoted in Cochran-Smith, 2004, p. xii).

I was willing to admit my own complicity in a racist society, but I found I lacked the theoretical tools necessary to clarify my understanding of the complexities of race to a degree that allowed me to guide my students out of a quagmire of resistance, defensiveness, and confusion. Needing help, I turned first to multicultural education and found Nieto (1999), Banks (1997), and others who challenged us to move toward a transformational approach to critical multicultural education (Sleeter & Grant, 2003).

Most literature on multiculturalism in art education was less helpful during my early years in Milwaukee, although there were exceptional art educators whose work was important to my development, including Desai (2003) and Gude (2000). Art education scholarship focused mainly on a pre-critical form of multiculturalism, simply a celebration of diversity (Chalmers, 1999). Since then, there has been a growing movement among art educators. 2010 saw a wave of interest in social justice. It was the theme for the National Art Education Association annual convention and the focus of a special edition of *Art Education* and an edited book: *Art Education for Social Justice* (Anderson, Gussak, Hallmark, & Paul, 2010). However, when I was searching for support I found art educators calling for a more inclusive framing of content but not addressing social justice or urban education issues.

An early and amazing discovery was Rethinking Schools, an independent nonprofit publisher based in Milwaukee. I found *Rethinking Schools* publications very helpful because they deal with issues of racism in ways that were accessible to my students. They are grounded in a critical theoretical foundation that was a lifesaver in my earlier years in Milwaukee. I continue to use them today.

Next, I discovered scholarship on culturally relevant pedagogy (Howard, 2003; Ladson-Billings, 1994, 2001). Up to that point, Delpit (1995) was one of my few references where this literature was concerned. According to Gay (2000), culturally relevant pedagogy uses "the cultural knowledge, prior experiences, frames of reference, and performance styles of ethnically diverse students to make learning more . . . effective" (p. 29). Through this body of research my students and I were better able to articulate a way toward understanding diverse learners.

Delving into culturally relevant pedagogy led me to scholarship on anti-racist teaching (Johnson, 2006; Kailin, 2002; Lee, Menkart, & Okazawa-Rey, 2006; Tatum, 1997). Distinct from, yet related to, critical multiculturalism and culturally relevant pedagogy, anti-racist teaching calls into question traditional practices of teacher education (Cochran-Smith, 2006). I felt like I was really onto something useful because it carries with it an activist imperative. With anti-racist teaching I felt I had a theoretical tool kit to begin to answer students who complained that they only wanted to know the tricks of the trade. Yet there was still something missing.

Finally, I stumbled into the terrain of whiteness studies (Jay, 2007; Kandiswamy, 2008; McIntosh, 1990; Thompson, 1997; Wise, 2008). According to Thompson (2003), "Whiteness theory does not address whiteness as a question of racial guilt or innocence based on skin color but as a system of privileges that is maintained discursively, institutionally, and materially" (2008). Investigations in whiteness studies have helped me and my students understand how White privilege transparently positions as Other those who are not White, while keeping itself invisible because of the way our culture is constructed.

According to McIntosh (1990), White people are meant to be oblivious to White privilege, which is "like an invisible weightless knapsack of special provisions" (p. 31). McIntosh goes on to say, "Whites are taught to think of their lives as morally neutral, normative, and average, and also ideal, so that when we work to benefit others, this is seen as work which will allow 'them' to be more like 'us.'" In whiteness studies, I had finally found a powerful way to illuminate the unacknowledged connections between my students and urban children of color.

Johnson (2006) takes the notion of privilege a few steps further to include socially constructed categories such as sexual orientation, gender, and disability.

Johnson's work can be connected to queer theory (Sullivan, 2003) and disability studies (Corker & Shakespeare, 2002; Eisenhauer, 2008) to bring students to a fuller understanding of the spectrum of privilege.

Through this expanded view of privilege, I can help students begin to see through circumstances they had taken for granted, such as the fact that children of color are identified for special education in far greater relative numbers than are white children. Systems they assume to be given are called into question, such as the myth of meritocracy in the United States (which claims that everyone has an equal chance to succeed if they work hard). To be effective teachers of urban children and youth, students must come to see that the status quo is not a neutral fact of life.

This theoretical journey has helped me to help my students develop a more rich and nuanced understanding of teaching in urban schools. With my theoretical toolkit in hand, I continue to walk with my students over the unsteady terrain of urban art teacher education—we do so with our eyes straining to seek justice.

Putting Theory into Practice: My Journey Continues

In this section I discuss facets of the art education program that has grown out of my search for understanding described above. In this evolutionary and revolutionary work, I am privileged to be joined by amazing colleagues. Together we ask students to engage in frank self-reflection with regard to race, class, gender, sexuality, and other markers of identity that impact schooling. We aim to help our students learn to recognize and challenge deeply engrained biases with the ultimate goal of developing an emancipatory, democratic teaching stance and culturally responsive, anti-biased pedagogy. Although there are myriad ways our art education program could be considered, I have developed three broad, interconnected thematic categories below: (1) Understanding Self, (2) Understanding Diverse Learners, and (3) Understanding Cultural Complexity.

Understanding Self

Learning to challenge entrenched ways of thinking about cultural differences is vital to teaching for social justice. Yet, like the majority of students in teacher preparation programs throughout the United States, our students come to us quite unaware of the ways their own concepts of identity work in relation to cultural others. They often say they have no culture or ethnicity because they see whiteness as the norm. About the intellectual and psychological work White people must do to be anti-racist, Lee stated:

> You need to look at your culture, what your idea of normal is, and realize it is quite limited and is in fact just reflecting a particular experience. You have to realize that what you recognize as universal is quite often exclusionary. (Lee in B. Miner, 1994/2000)

Without doing so consciously, white people make people who are different from them abnormal. To work against this, we develop opportunities for our students to reflect on their own identities in relation to the broader cultural milieu in which they will be teaching.

Teaching autobiographies, or teacher narratives, can be powerful tools for both novice and practicing teachers to engage in focused and purposeful self-reflection (Cochran-Smith, 2004; Nieto, 2003). Students regularly develop self-reflective practices from very early in their course of studies. These include online reflective journals that respond to Wisconsin's teaching standards and visual journals, which are more artful and autobiographical (New, 2005; Trafi-Prats, personal communication, September 14, 2008). Using these powerful learning tools, situated within an inquiry- and field-based program, our students write about and illustrate their journeys into the art teaching profession in order to develop a habit of self-reflective praxis.

We ask them to reflect on their autobiographies as a way to open conversations about identity with regard to readings connected to whiteness studies, critical theory, critical multicultural education, and anti-racist teaching in relation to local and national education issues. In this way, we are able to challenge the tendencies they have to take matters of identity for granted.

In concert with the journals, we ask students to interrogate teacher identity through a variety of visual projects. For example, we've asked students to create photomontages/collages based on the work of Hannah Höch and Martha Rosler as a way to consider the multidimensional nature of identity. Focusing on the work of contemporary artists such as Majane Satrapi (2003), as well as the comic book of *To Teach* by William Ayers and Ryan Alexander Tanner (2010), students have made comics and illustrations to represent, among other things, alter egos making a difference in unjust situations in which they had felt powerless in real life.

We discuss the social construction of teacher identity through media and popular culture, such as the savior/teacher in *Precious* (Daniels, 2009) and Taylor Mali's slam poem *What Teachers Make* (2002). As part of this investigation, we asked students to do drawings and reflections of memorable teachers in their visual journals. Using these drawings as a jumping-off point, they created puppets of their teacher characters. During the time they worked on the puppets on their own, we worked through readings that brought forward issues connected with power, privilege, and difference. Toward the end of the semester, students created puppet plays that dealt with issues that had arisen throughout the class. In this way, we were able to wrestle with big ideas and work through some tough issues while taking the edge off the difficulty of such dialogue. Through such artful activities, our students engage in deep thinking about identity, justice, and power in a manner that is comfortable for them. Depth of reflection has risen over time as we have changed our curriculum to include more identity-focused experiences.

The growth in students' self-reflection in their portfolios suggests to us that this type of art-based research and engagement with ideas is paying off.

Understanding Diverse Learners

When learning about children's artistic development pre-service teachers usually learn that children and youth move through various stages in which roughly the same sorts of visual information appear over time (Lowenfeld & Brittain, 1975). While we believe it is good for students to see that there are similarities across different children, they must understand, as well, that these stages are also cultural artifacts. In order to best prepare students to work with diverse learners, then, we believe it is important to link artistic development to other theories of social and cultural development and to culturally relevant, anti-biased, critical pedagogy.

In addition to thinking about artistic development through social and cultural prisms, we feel it is important for each pre-service teacher to develop a strong relationship with a group of urban children. Toward that end, we've established partnerships with several schools in our area. Our students' first early field experience is different from most I know about, in that it takes place in a general education classroom rather than an art room. We do this for several reasons. First, it allows us to split our 30-student cohort into 2 working groups, each supervised by a faculty member (we team-teach our upper-level classes, which are combined theory and practice courses that count for 6 credits apiece). This arrangement allows us to set aside 2 full days per week to integrate in-class work and school-based early field experience. In both schools there is a dynamic art teacher who coordinates the partnership with the faculty member.

Second, in addition to logistical expediency, we believe this arrangement provides important spaces for students to develop strong bonds within a school community. Faculty members also develop bonds with teachers and students over time because they work in the same school every fall semester. In this way, we faculty members have opportunities to model relational, community-centered, culturally relevant pedagogy for our students.

There is a large body of research showing that effective teachers of students of color, white teachers and teachers of color alike, form and maintain connections with students within their social contexts. They understand their students as individuals and as members of specific communities. They ask students to share who they are and what they know with the class in a variety of ways. They regularly incorporate instructional materials that provide various viewpoints from different cultures. These teachers exhibit an anti-biased, culturally responsive pedagogy that is the basis for social justice work in any educational context (Cochran-Smith, 2006; Irvine, 1997; Ladson-Billings, 1994).

For most students, working for social justice is not a high priority when they enter our program. To successfully ignite a spark for change, we must teach them while they work with children with whom they can build a connection. Our students usually go into the 1st day of the field experience with fear and trepidation (as I did when I first stepped into a Milwaukee public school). But by the end of the experience, they are sad to leave; each usually has in her or his teaching philosophy some version of my second rule: If you treat students like human beings, regardless of reputation or stereotype, they usually live up to your expectations.

Understanding Cultural Complexity

While it is often necessary to convince students that working for social justice in teaching is important, most usually embrace the idea with time. However, if we ended there we would be doing them, and their future students, a grave injustice, for they must also be mindful that if they are to actually go out in the world and make a difference, they must come to understand the barriers that can stand in the way of teaching in urban schools. This is, perhaps, where the theoretical foundations of our program most support us. If our students are to be reasonably expected to go out into the world to create social change, they must comprehend the "whys" of phenomena such as the effects of low expectations on children of color and poor white children. Similarly, they must be able to spot the subtle forms of discrimination inherent in institutionalized racism, homophobia, and other forms of oppression as they relate to the complex web of schools and culture. Through readings, discussions, research, and reflection we strive to prepare our students to recognize the interplay of power, privilege, and difference in Milwaukee and beyond so they can challenge the status quo through meaningful curriculum and relational instruction.

Students must come to see that organizing for change takes more than youthful exuberance; it takes dogged persistence and a willingness to forgo instant gratification. Teachers who make a difference work to create democratic school cultures, even if those cultures function only in a few teachers' classrooms inside a larger, more traditional school. It is important to know how to seek out others who share a desire for justice by joining groups such as the Educators' Network for Social Justice (www.ensj.org), by attending curriculum fairs such as those hosted by Teachers for Social Justice (http://www.teachersforjustice.org/), and by supporting organizations such as Rethinking Schools (http://www.rethinkingschools.org/) and Teaching Tolerance (www.teachingtoleracne.org), which publish resources that will keep hope alive in the face of the inevitable adversity they will encounter in urban schools. With the support of like-minded colleagues, new teachers and seasoned teachers alike can keep pessimism at bay and be mindful that in order to teach for social justice, you must not succumb to cynicism; rather, you must train your eyes to see the possible. By training our eyes to see the possible through purposeful self-reflection; ongoing efforts to understand why injustice occurs and what must be done to make change; and connecting with community members, including other artists and teachers who imagine a better life for urban teachers and students, we can stand together to see that the possible happens in urban schools.

REFERENCES

Anderson, T., Gussak, D., Hallmark, K. K., & Paul, A. (2010). *Art education for social justice.* Reston, VA: National Art Education Association.

Ayers, W. (2004). *Teaching towards freedom: Moral commitment and ethical action in the classroom.* Boston, MA: Beacon Press.

Ayers, W., & Alexander-Tanner, R. (2010). *To teach: The journey, in comics.* New York: Teachers College Press

Ayers, W., Quinn, T., & Stovall, D. (2009). *Handbook of social justice in education.* New York: Routledge.

Banks, J. (1997). *Educating citizens in a multicultural society.* New York: Teachers College Press.

Chalmers, F. G. (1999). *Celebrating cultural pluralism: Multicultural approaches to art learning.* Los Angeles, CA: Getty Education Institute for the Arts.

Cochran-Smith, M. (2004). *Walking the road: Race, diversity, and social justice in teacher education.* New York: Teachers College Press.

Cochran-Smith, M. (2006). Ten promising trends (and three big worries). *Educational Leadership, 63*(6), 20–25.

Collins, G., & Sandell, R. (1984). *Women, art, and education.* Reston, VA: National Art Education Association.

Collins, G., & Sandell, R. (1996). *Gender issues in art education: Content, contexts, and strategies.* Reston, VA: National Art Education Association.

Corker, M., & Shakespeare, T. (Eds.). (2002). *Disability/postmodernity: Embodying disability theory.* New York: Continuum.

Cosier, K. (2010). The bearded mother rides shotgun: On being intellectual offspring of Dr. Enid Zimmerman. In R. Sabol & M. Manifold (Eds.), *Through the prism: Looking into the spectrum of writings by Enid Zimmerman* (pp. 313–332). Reston, VA: National Art Education Association.

Daniels, L. (Director/Producer). (2009). *Precious: Based on the novel "Push" by Sapphire* [Motion Picture]. United States: Lionsgate.

Delpit, L. (1995). *Other people's children: Cultural conflict in the classroom.* New York: The New Press.

Desai, D. (2003). Multicultural education and the heterosexual imagination: A question of culture. *Studies in Art Education, 44*(2), 147–161.

Dobbs, S. M. (1992). *The DBAE handbook: An overview of Discipline-Based Art Education.* Los Angeles: Getty Center for Education in the Arts.

Eisenhauer, J. (2008). A visual culture of stigma: Critically examining representations of mental illness. *Art Education, 61*(5), 13–18.

Ellsworth, E. (1989). Why doesn't this feel empowering? Working through the repressive myths of critical pedagogy. *Harvard Educational Review, 59*(3), 297–324.

Fehr, D., Fehr, K., & Kiefer-Boyd, K. (Eds). (2000). *Real world readings in art education: Things your professors never told you.* New York: Falmer Press.

Freire, P. (1970). *Pedagogy of the oppressed*. New York: Continuum.

Garber, E. (1996). Art criticism from a feminist point of view: An approach for teachers. In G. Collins & R. Sandell (Eds.), *Gender issues in art education: Content, contexts and strategies* (pp. 21–29). Reston, VA: National Art Education Association.

Gaudelius, Y. (2000). Feminist and critical pedagogies: Intersections and divergences. In D. Fehr, K. Fehr, & K. Kiefer-Boyd (Eds.), *Real world readings in art education: Things your professors never told you* (pp. 21–27). New York: Falmer Press.

Gay, G. (2000). *Culturally responsive teaching: Theory, research, & practice*. New York: Teachers College Press.

Giroux, H. A., & McLaren, P. L. (Eds.). (1989). *Critical pedagogy, the state, and cultural struggle*. Albany, NY: State University of New York Press.

Gramsci, A. (1971). *Selections from the prison notebooks*. London: Lawrence and Wishart.

Greene, M. (1988). *The dialectic of freedom*. New York: Teachers College Press.

Gude, O. (2000). Investigating the culture of curriculum. In D. Fehr, K. Fehr, & K. Kiefer-Boyd (Eds.), *Real world readings in art education: Things your professors never told you* (pp. 75–81). New York: Falmer Press.

hooks, b. (1994). *Teaching to transgress: Education as the practice of freedom*. New York: Routledge.

Howard, T. C. (2003). Culturally relevant pedagogy: Ingredients for critical teacher reflection. *Theory Into Practice, 42*(3), 195–202.

Irvine, J. (Ed.). (1997). *Constructing the knowledge base for urban teacher education*. Washington, DC: American Association of Colleges for Teacher Education.

Jay, G. (2007). Who invented white people? In R. P. Yagleski (Ed.), *The Thompson reader: Conversations in context* (pp. 96–102). Boston: Thompson/Heinle.

Johnson, A. (2006). *Privilege, power, and difference*. New York: McGraw-Hill.

Kailin, J. (2002). *Anti-racist education: From theory to practice*. Lanham, MD: Rowman & Littlefield.

Kandiswamy, P. (2008). Beyond colorblindness and multiculturalism: Rethinking anti-racist pedagogy in the university classroom. *Radical Teacher, 80*, 6–11.

Kozol, J. (1991). *Savage inequalities: Children in America's schools*. New York: Crown.

Ladson-Billings, G. (1994). *The dreamkeepers: Successful teachers of African American children*. San Francisco, CA: Jossey-Bass.

Ladson-Billings, G. (2001). *Crossing over to Canaan: The journey of new teachers in diverse classrooms*. San Francisco, CA: Jossey-Bass.

Lareau, A. (1989). *Home advantage: Social class and parental intervention in elementary education*. London: Falmar Press.

Lather, P. (1998). Critical pedagogy and its complicities. *Educational Theory, 48*(4), 487–497.

Lee, E., Menkart, D., & Okazawa-Rey, M. (Eds.). (2006). *Beyond heroes and holidays: A practical guide to K–12 anti-racist, multicultural education and staff development*. Washington, DC: Teaching For Change.

Lowenfeld, Brittain, W. L. (1975). *Creative and mental growth*. New York: Macmillan.

Mali, T. (2002). *What teachers make*. Retrieved from http://www.taylormali.com/index.cfm?webid=13.

McClaren, P. (1989). *Life in schools: An introduction to critical pedagogy in the foundations of education*. New York: Longman.

McIntosh, P. (1990). White privilege: Unpacking the invisible knapsack. *Independent School*, *49*(2), 31–36.

Miner, B. (1994/2000). Taking multicultural, anti-racist education seriously: An interview with Enid Lee. *Rethinking Our Classrooms*, (*1*), 15–17. Milwaukee, WI: Rethinking Schools.

New, J. (2005). *Drawing from life: The journal as art*. New York: Princeton Architectural Press.

Nieto, S. (1999). *The light in their eyes: Creating multicultural learning communities*. New York: Teachers College Press.

Nieto, S. (2003). *What keeps teachers going?* New York: Teachers College Press.

Nochlin, L. (1971, January). Why have there been no great women artists? *ARTnews, 69*, 22–39, 67–71.

Noddings, N. (1992). *The challenge to care in schools: An alternative approach to education*. New York: Teachers College Press.

Pollock, G. (1992). *Vision and difference: Femininity, feminism, and histories of art*. London: Routledge and New York: Methuen. (Routledge Classic edition 2004)

Pollock, G. (1996). *Generations and geographies: Critical theories and critical practices in feminism and the visual arts*. New York: Routledge.

Pollock, G. (2007). *Conceptual odysseys: Passages to cultural analysis*. London: I. B. Tauris.

Satrapi, M. (2003). *Persepolis: The story of a childhood*. New York: Pantheon.

Sleeter, C. E., & Grant, C. A. (2003). *Making choices for multicultural education: Five approaches to race, class, and gender*. New York: John Wiley & Sons.

Sullivan, N. (2003). *A critical introduction to queer theory*. New York: New York University Press.

Tatum, B. D. (1997). *"Why are all the Black kids sitting together in the cafeteria?" and other conversations about race*. New York: Basic Books.

Thompson, A. (1997). For: Anti-racist education. *Curriculum Inquiry, 27*(1), 7–44.

Thompson, A. (2003). *Whiteness theory and education*. Retrieved from http://www .pauahtun.org/6624-7624.F03.html.

Wise, T. (2008). *White like me: Reflections on race from a privileged son*. Brooklyn, NY: Soft Skull Press.

Zimmerman, E., co-edited with E. Sacca. (1998). *Women art educators IV: Her stories, our stories, future stories*. Montreal, Canada: Canadian Society for Education through Art.

5

The City as a Culturally Quilted Pedagogical Territory

LEDA GUIMARÃES

> The city should be viewed as a plural and multifaceted organization. It is
> a multiple set of collective actions elaborated in several dimensions, very
> meaningful and able to build identities and identifications. In a single space in
> the city are found different actors and organizations simultaneously playing
> their roles.
>
> —Paulo César Rodrigues Carrano, *Juventudes e Cidades Educadoras*,
> translation by author

Like many teacher educators, I am engaged in developing teachers' skills in a contemporary scenario, understanding the pedagogical as political and the political as pedagogical (Barbosa, 2006; Bastos, 2006; Daniel, 2005; Freire, 1996; Freedmam & Stuhr, 2009). Using a metaphor of the city as culturally quilted pedagogical territory, in which urban identity is made up of a patchwork of cultural traditions and polyphonic, socially built spaces, helps students who plan to teach in urban settings come to understand the complexity of their cultural arenas. In this way they come to understand a quilted territory comprised of conflicted spaces and diverse living experiences that, when interweaved, generate new meanings.

Cities have long had histories of patchwork cultures, but realms of the political and the pedagogical have expanded with globalization, which has brought the idea of the global cultural supermarket, coupled with fascination with (and fear of) *difference and local culture.* In contemporary cities, new identities result from increased transit between global and local spheres. Living in urban spaces can overthrow fixed identities, in part because a multiplicity of cultural aspects builds a complex fabric of information and behaviors. Bastos (2006) argues that our goal should be "to prepare art educators to learn how to inquire about art and culture and investigate the dialectics of local and global influences within a particular context. Such research can inform meaningful art education" (p. 20).

Aguirre (2010) affirms that urban education has taken on increasing importance as the world's population has shifted to cities. One aspect of this contemporary scenario is the concern for preparing students for urban education as a critical teaching practice. These seem to me to be very intriguing reasons for considering the city as a scenario in which educators can engage with aesthetic experiences connected to a complex and plural world. Such an approach to urban teacher education can spark fascination with diverse local cultures and ameliorate fears of difference. Toward that end, this chapter is organized to (1) provide a conceptual framework for understanding urban art teacher education as a culturally quilted pedagogical space, (2) examine the goals, structure, and context of a student-led research project, and (3) analyze its outcomes and discuss implications for an approach to the preparation and professional development of art educators that is attuned to the issues of our contemporary global society.

UNDERSTANDING URBAN ART EDUCATION IN A CULTURALLY QUILTED TERRITORY

The city, a living and dynamic territory, can be a source for educators' praxis, changing closed notions about education toward perspectives that link together daily life and visual culture. In contrast, about traditional processes of education Jurjo Santomé (1998) states:

> Curriculum and contents that are developed in most of the school systems emphasize the so-called hegemonic cultures. Cultures or voices of minorities and/or marginalized social groups that do not own powerful important structures are usually silenced. In fact, one of the most important existing gaps is the reflection of the true meaning of different cultures of races or ethnicity. It is precisely in moments like the ones we have been living, where problems will arise because different races and ethnicities will share and be in the same territory, that this emptiness will be deeply felt. (Santomé, 2001, p. 161, translation by author)

Taking the visualities of the city as a starting point for curriculum development can help bridge differences and fill the empty spaces about which Santomé writes. In my research (Guimarães, 2005, 2007), I have investigated urban visualities, including such things as billboards, graffiti, public art, daily objects, commercial storefronts, diverse architectural solutions, and much more. Investigating such urban visualities unveils interconnected narratives of ordinary experience and can be an approach to community-based pedagogy (Daniel, 2005), which can serve as a means of connecting teachers, community members, and students through educational cultural practices.

In developing this approach to urban teacher education, I sought to confront my students with the cultural complexities and hybrid situations learned through mapping urban visualities that mark daily life on cities. At the same time, I hoped to prompt self-reflection and critical analysis of teaching art education through visual culture practices. Freedman and Stuhr (2009) state, "The current transformation of art education is more than just a broadening of curriculum content and changes in teaching strategies in response to the immediacy and mass distribution of imagery" (p. 11). Thus we can say that seeing the city as rich with possibilities for art education is part of a larger movement that needs a "new level of theorizing about art in education that is tied to emergent postmodern philosophies based on this growing environment of intercultural, intracultural, and transcultural visualizations" (Freedman & Stuhr, 2009, p. 11).

Suzi Gablik (2002), an American artist and writer, has advocated an attitude about contemporary art based on its possibility of re-enchantment. One of the rationales of her proposal is the transition from an aesthetic of individuality to an aesthetic of interconnectivity, with attendant social responsibility and ecological commitment. According to Gablik, this transition sets a new paradigm related to the concept of ecology, which in turn corresponds to a holistic comprehension of the space in which we are inserted. A holistic attitude unites inside and outside worlds—subjective and objective—in a unified perception. When this perception is experienced in different sociocultural contexts, we are no longer observers; instead we become determining factors in the process of building realities.

I use Gablik's interconnectivity point of view (2002) to justify the need to re-enchant the teaching of art. My idea is to think about the city as a scenario for educational performances and as a base from which to teach art pedagogy in a contemporary way. Such an approach suggests an ethnographic basis for teacher education in order to develop inquiry abilities, visual explorations, and open minds to the diverse narratives inherent in a city. In this way, the conception of city as a culturally quilted pedagogical territory gives us a framework to discuss an asset-based approach to urban teacher education that addresses the political and the pedagogical.

EXPLORING THE CULTURAL QUILT OF A CITY THROUGH STUDENT-LED CURRICULUM RESEARCH

My goal was to design a project that would create a model of curriculum development focused on the culturally quilted pedagogical territory of neighborhoods in our city, Goiânia, Brazil, with a group of art education students who worked with Visual Arts Faculty at the Universidade Federal de Goiás (UFG). Goiânia was founded to be the capital of Goiás State on October 24, 1933. It is located in the central plateau, 209 kilometers from Brasilia, the capital of Brazil. The city has more than one million inhabitants. Goiânia was born as a symbol of modernity and progress. Being a very young city, and strategically located in the heart of the Central West Region, Goiânia attracts migrants from all regions of Brazil. The young city has beautiful parks interrupting the urban landscape, thus providing a modern capital with a pleasant quality of life. Many of the first large buildings of the city center were built in an Art Deco style, between the 1940s and 1950s, and constitute a significant collection from the standpoint of the history of Brazilian architecture.

The project, called *Bairro, Escola, Universidade* (Neighborhood, School, University), challenged students to engage in an internship with a school partner, by way of exploring a particular neighborhood in Goiânia. After mapping and immersing themselves in the culture of the neighborhood, each group of students chose a space for pedagogical action. During these site visits, the students' investigation of the sites pursued these essential questions: How are these spaces visually characterized? What are the iconographies present in the urban environment? Who makes the images exposed to the public in a recurring way? Whom do those images serve? What are these images for? How do we interact (or not) with different visualities? How can we bring them into the context of teaching to a visual culture art education? These questions were designed to help students begin a transition from the homogeneity of their own experience toward a critical understanding of diversity and embracing the right to live with difference.

Students collected data by following a research plan in order to 1) justify why the neighborhood was chosen, 2) describe the aim of the research, 3) show street mapping, and 4) report on interviews with people living in the community. In this way, the students begin to see neighborhoods as "regular places" with social obligations driving the daily life of those who live there. From an endless data field, students were instructed to focus on one site in one neighborhood in an attempt to understand the complex Brazilian imaginary contained in its visual culture.

A NEIGHBORHOOD BRIDE SPARKS A RESEARCH AND TEACHING PROJECT

Figure 5.1 is one example that demonstrates the interconnection proposed between neighborhood, school, and university, conceptualizing the city as a quilted pattern of art practices, aesthetics, and cultural contexts. The group of students who chose this site consisted of four women who had already attended the Graphic Design program at UFG. Thus, they had already completed the academic requirements to carry out an investigative project. Where they lacked experience was within educational contexts. So their ideas about art as a content area and their notions about being art teachers were based on traditional rules of art history and their experiences with behavior models for classrooms inside schools. Through this project, however, their understandings of both content and pedagogy were expanded as they researched a neighborhood called Setor Pedro Ludovico and developed a curriculum based on their research. Built in the early 1950s, the Setor Pedro Ludovico neighborhood is situated in the southern part of Goiania. It is a place where migrants moved from the country's northeast. Such was the trajectory of Pedro (for

Figure 5.1. A neighborhood bride.

whom the neighborhood is named), who migrated from Alagoas, a northeastern state beset by drought. Once settled in Goiania, he became a community leader welcoming families, mostly from the northeast. The community that has grown there has resisted threats and survived great difficulties. The ancient name "macambira," a native plant from northeastern Brazil well known for its resistance capacity, is used as a nickname for the neighborhood because it signifies the strength of survival and beauty found there. In Macambira the walls are full of billboards, artistic posters, graffiti, public signs, and other forms of visual culture.

While the group of four students captured visual and historical data about Macambira, they encountered a wedding dress shop on whose outer wall was a painting of a bride. Intrigued by this painting, the students decided to dig deeper. They learned that the owners of the shop are Wanderley Guimarães[1] and his wife, Sofia, the daughter of a Polish resistance fighter who came to Goiania fleeing the Nazis during World War II. At that time, Wanderley and his father had belonged to the municipal guard. One night, they were called to help a foreign family newly arrived in the settlement. No one in the family could speak Portuguese, but Wanderley could see that young Sophia was very sick. He took the girl to the only hospital in town; her case was urgent, but Wanderley had no money, so Sophia was refused care. Overcome by his desire to help the young Polish girl, Wanderley drew his weapon, aimed it at the hospital personnel, and demanded that they provide care. Less than 3 months later they married.

The couple opened the shop together. Every year Wanderley and Sofia organize the largest collective wedding ceremony in the country, with 300 couples participating annually. The event is broadcast by Globo, one of the major television networks in Brazil. Sofia reported that putting on the mass wedding provides a dream space of the ideal wedding for young couples, with all production supported by their shop: dresses, bouquets, hair designs, and makeup. Sofia and Wanderley say the idea came to them years ago when women who lacked financial means to buy the expensive dresses would come into their shop, stare at the albums, and sigh, "If only . . ." Sofia and Wanderley wanted to make that dream possible. After hearing their marriage history and stories of the mass weddings, the students discovered that the community had many other intercultural love stories. For example, the students found out that Inácio, the painter of the bride advertisement, came from another state, and followed his wife to Macambira, where she was from.

Among the many possibilities in the neighborhood, these students chose the bride painting, and hence all patterns came together as a starting point of a pedagogical intervention. The image of the bride sparked an interest, but the structure of the project helped them to learn a great deal more. With these narratives in mind, my students followed through on the second part of the course assignment by going to the local school to explain an initial idea and convince teachers and other school personnel to engage in the community-based art project. They made the following proposal submitted by Noeli Batista and translated by author:

- Find out if people in the community know about the bride mural.
- Tell the story about the family of the shop's founders, develop a drawing and collage workshop, and introduce "Inácio's bride."
- Show images of weddings using several sources: fine arts, popular and commercial art, and so on.
- Use pictures of weddings and personal statements from the trainees and the target group.
- Discuss the differences and similarities among the images.
- Discuss the role of women in marriage.
- Discuss how images reveal ideological changes, behavioral transformations, ways of domination, and so on.
- Obtain new images in order to design a panel about the topic, having Inácio as instructor/assistant.
  (Noeli Batista, 2006, translated by author)

Members of the school community were interested in their ideas, and a group of teachers and other school employees formed to develop this pedagogical practice further in the school. After the group engaged in research about the site, Inácio, the painter of the bride, was invited to teach a class on mural art whose theme was marriage and memory.

ANALYSIS OF THE OUTCOMES

The arts workshops promoted research, production, and manipulation of images to develop a critical understanding of urban neighborhood visualities. Issues such as gender hierarchies, identity, and subjectivity were brought up in the inquiry exercise; for example, some wedding photographs fostered questions such as: Why was the woman seated and the man standing with his hand on the shoulder of the bride? And why was a technical treatment to lighten skin used in a picture of a Black couple? At the end of the workshops participants made statements about their engagement with the neighborhood and how their perspectives had changed. One woman shared that before this experience she had walked like a pig, head down, staring at the floor. But now she looked up to connect with the many images around her. Starting from one local advertisement, my students and their school partners gained insight into wider cultural questions. The outcomes of this study demonstrate that educators who expand their vision by placing it in the context of the quilted visual culture of the city can promote socialization of knowledge and culture as living experiences of learning practice and reflection. Working within this ethnographic approach broadened my students' perspectives beyond what is possible in a traditional culturally hegemonic curriculum, which is based on fine art history. Piecing together aspects of neighborhood and family culture, traditions and habits, gives students the fabric that makes up the whole of the cultural quilt. This approach has changed their perspectives about the city and about teaching urban youth. It has given them an intellectually engaging source of art and culturally relevant content from which to create a new kind of curriculum.

My students related that the bride painting first drew their attention for its artistic quality and visual impact. However, with the progress of the project they came to understand that the image's meaning was linked to the space and to the narratives of the people who inhabit the space. The union of art and social spaces is central to this approach to art pedagogy. Here, the image of the bride, the space of the shop, and the history of its inhabitants come together in an interesting perspective for a project of teaching art. Using the urban space as a framework to teach art, the emphasis is on how the practice might be more significant when considering and understanding the patterns related to art, culture, and the community.

As noted, the task of developing teachers' skills in a contemporary scenario includes understanding the pedagogical as political and the political as pedagogical (Freire, 1996). The students' experiences in *Bairro, Escola, Universidade*

(Neighborhood, School, University) resulted in conceptual disruptions that caused them to rethink the performance of art educators in contemporaneity. They experienced a transition from an indifferent gaze to a reflective one that inquires and integrates.

This process of encountering an urban space is the challenge in the education of visual art teachers, who think of the school only as a physical space to educate people, segregated from the world outside. This "outside" world is the space where young people achieve most of their artistic, aesthetic, and cultural repertoire. In the final section, I will link our experiences in *Bairro, Escola, Universidade* (Neighborhood, School, University) to the framework of the cultural quilt and theorize possible broad implications for art teacher education and professional development as a political act.

IMPLICATIONS FOR PRACTICE

This approach to the preparation and professional development of art educators is attuned to issues of our contemporary global society. It points to growth that can take place for pre-service teachers and school community members, but also to the need for university faculty to engage with the city and invest in transforming actions that build realities connected to contemporary life. Hence, I propose an ecological learning approach to the city, trying to discover the city inside and outside each one of us. In this regard, I walk along with other art educators (Bastos & Hutzel, 2004) who practice asset-based community art curriculum by engaging with the city.

Expanding the field is not enough; instead we need to question the education of future teachers in terms of contemporary issues and contexts. The conception of city as a culturally quilted pedagogical territory allows us to think about its crossings and conflicts, and the unterritorialization and reterritorialization of its spaces, giving us a context in which to discuss an asset-based approach to teacher education. This means that there is a need to rethink the performance of those who are responsible for what the university is like, promoting actions that are able to break crystallized curriculum models, interconnecting them to the transformations that occur in contemporaneity. Working toward re-dimensioning future educators implies re-dimensioning ourselves and leveraging other ways of thinking and practicing teacher education.

Using the complex and multifaceted urban quilt, educators can become co-editors of the individual and collective narrations that are interwoven with the visual, incorporating artistic and aesthetic learning that is different from pre-established manuals or books of fine art. This urban fabric shows other logics that are not perceived in the institutionalized educational context and require different daily strategies, which can be summarized as follows:

- *Mappings and cartographies:* The construction of ethnographic skills is fundamental to penetrating the urban context. Reflecting about the city and its plurality of cultural practices also means that we have to be prepared to elect (and reelect) routes.
- *Managing meanings:* In order to go inside the city's patchwork, skill is required to perceive different actors, the roles they play, their conflicts, and positions of power. Such work requires that we come to understand that urban visualities can have multiple, overlapping meanings that are connected to representations of what people make of themselves and of others, and events that give life meaning.
- *Flexibility of intentions:* Immersion in diverse neighborhood spaces demands flexibility in the construction and management of pedagogical mediations. Plans need constant reorientations.
- *Building partnerships:* Considering the city as a quilted learning scenario requires the association of partners, facing problems and searching for answers through different knowledge and competences. Such engagement can move us from an aesthetic of individuality to an aesthetic of interconnectivity, with attendant social responsibility and ecological commitment (Gablik, 2002).
- *Editing narratives:* This ethnographic practice helps build critical reflective practice, with the goal of pointing to how symbolic systems enable knowledge and also aggregate interpretative signs of the urban space so that they can be associated with the practice of teaching visual arts.

The notion of a city as a culturally quilted territory implies polyphonic, socially built spaces. The metaphor of the city as a cultural patchwork helps us understand the challenge of being educators in an era where the framework for subjectivity and sociability is different than in the past, and is formed in mainly urban contexts. This idea of a cultural patchwork does not show a consensus. On the contrary, the concept of "cities as cultural arenas" acknowledges that

> urban communication is a result of the multi-cultural dialogue among heterogenic subjects. In these dialogues, there is a struggle among the ones in an antagonist position, fighting for territories and meanings; there is solidarity to perform common interests and also indifference shown by those who isolate themselves in the deaf dialogue of a city of privations that markets command. (Carrano, 2003, p. 24)

People who plan to teach in urban settings must come to understand the complexity of their cultural arenas, to see that quilted territory is comprised of conflicted spaces and living experiences that, when interweaved, generate new meanings. The concern for preparing students for urban education as a critical teaching practice is particularly compelling at a time when more people live in cities than ever and realms of the political and the pedagogical have expanded with globalization. These seem to me to be very intriguing reasons for considering the city as a culturally quilted pedagogical territory, a scenario in which educators can engage with aesthetic experiences connected to a complex and plural world.

NOTE

1. Despite having the same last name, Wanderley and Sofia Guimarães are not relatives of the author.

REFERENCES

Aguirre, I. (2010). *Questões Multiculturais para o ensino da arte* [Multicultural issues for art education]. Licenciatura em Artes Visuais: módulo 7/Universidade Federal de Goiás, Faculdade de Artes Visuais. Goiânia: FUNAPE, 2010. 213.

Barbosa, A. M. (org.). (2006). *Consonâncias internacionais para o ensino da arte* [Contemporary art/education: International consonances]. Cortez: São Paulo.

Bastos, F. M. C. (2006). Border-crossing dialogues: Engaging art education students in cultural research. *Art Education, 59*(4), 20–24.

Bastos, F. M. C., & Hutzel, K. (2004). Art in the Market project: Addressing racial issues through community art. *Journal of Cultural Research in Art Education, 22,* 86–98.

Carrano, P. C. R. (2003). *Juventudes e cidades educadoras* [Youths and educating cities]. Petrópolis, RJ: Editora Vozes.

Daniel, V. (2005). Components of the community act as sources of pedagogy. *Visualidades: Revista do programa de mestrado em cultura visual/Faculdade de Artes Visuais/UFG* [Visualities: Journal of the Masters Program in Visual Culture], Vol. 3, n. 1.

Freire, P. (1996). *Pedagogia da autonomia: Saberes necessários à prática educativa* [Pedagogy of autonomy: Knowledge necessary for educational practice]. São Paulo, Brazil: Paz e Terra.

Freedman, K., & Stuhr, P. (2009, January/June). Curriculum change for the 21st century: Visual culture in art education. *VIS—Revista do programa de pós-graduação em arte, 8*(1), 9–22. Brasília: Editora Brasil.

Gablik, S. (2002). *The reenchantment of art.* New York: Thames & Hudson.

Guimarães, L. (2005). *Entre a universidade e a diversidade—a linha vermelha do ensino da arte* [Between the university and diversity—The red line of art teaching]. Tese de Doutorado. ECA-USP.

Guimarães, L. (2007). *Prática pedagógica em artes visuais—star point, game over or play again? Redimensionando a caminhada.* Anais Anpap. Florianpólis-SC.

Hutzel, K. (2007). Reconstructing a community, reclaiming a playground: A participatory action research study. *Studies in Art Education, 48*(3), 299–315.

Hyssen, A. (2008). *Other cities other worlds: Urban imaginaries in a globalizing age.* Durham, NC: Duke University Press.

Santomé, J. (1998). *Globalização e interdisciplinaridade: O currículo integrado* [Globalization and interdisciplinarity: The integrated curriculum]. Porto Alegre: Editora Artes Médicas Sul Ltda.

6

Community Arts Academy

Service Learning for Urban Art Teachers

DONALYN HEISE & BRYNA BOBICK

Teachers do not work in isolation, but as part of a greater community.
—Nicole Raymer Harper, "Influencing K12 Art Programs"

Teaching is like juggling—it requires handling multiple difficult feats with a large repertoire of knowledge and skills (Tredway, 1999). Urban education requires teachers to have habits of mind that support achievement, such as recognizing contributions of urban youth and having positive expectations for all students. We know teachers play a critical role in the success of students in urban environments, yet often feel ill prepared for the challenges they may face (Jacob, 2007; Quinn & Kahne, 2001). Some teachers enter certification programs having little experience with minority students and urban school environments (Jacob, 2007; Tredway, 1999). Yet pre-service teaching programs often focus on traditional pedagogical practices and do not address teaching art in urban settings. Thus, in order to better prepare students to teach art in urban settings, we created the Community Arts Academy, giving them opportunities to critically reflect on teaching and learning in an urban neighborhood and providing authentic experiences with a diverse student population.

This chapter examines lessons we have learned through the Community Arts Academy, a collaborative, service learning program providing teacher preparation and professional development in an urban community setting near the University of Memphis. We begin with an overview of our conceptual framework, which situates service learning within a frame of resilience theory. Next, we describe our neighborhood program, including its context and our approach to curriculum, which was executed through instructional play. Finally, to discuss what we have learned, we highlight the stories of Jillian, a 1st-year teacher/graduate student, and Kendal, an undergraduate art education major.[1]

A SERVICE LEARNING PROGRAM BUILT UPON A RESILIENCE THEORY FRAMEWORK

Service learning is a way for students to apply academic skills to real-life situations in their own communities (Payne, 2000; Taylor, 2002). It provides experiences that meet community needs, supports school and community collaboration, and allows learning to be extended beyond the classroom. Sometimes service learning is approached as a social action that stresses the need for collaborative self-transformation and creating a more just society (Hutzel, 2007; Pearson, 1999). The Community Art Academy is an example of a just such a program. Another example of an asset-based approach to art education is an art and literacy program for children in a homeless shelter, profiled by Heise and MacGillivray (2010), which focused on individual strengths, and was guided by children's self-identified assets of resourcefulness, creativity, and perseverance.

Through service learning activities, students can connect the information they learn in the school's curriculum with the wider world (Payne, 2000). Service learning projects involving art education students at the university level allow opportunities for authentic teaching and learning experiences that may not occur through traditional college teaching methods courses. In order to make service learning programs work for all participants, it is important to find a balance between skills provided by participants from the university and the skills of community members. We have found that this balance can be achieved through collaborative planning, flexibility, and recognizing the expertise of each person (Jeffers, 2005). We agree with Taylor (2002), who writes that service learning works best when students are provided structured time to reflect on their experiences.

The Community Arts Academy was a service learning program built upon a framework of resilience theory. Too often, urban youth are portrayed and labeled by their failures and risk factors, rather than their assets (Brendtro, Ness, & Mitchell, 2005; Jacob, 2007). Yet urban youth are often quite resilient, despite the many factors that work against them. They can be resourceful, perceptive, energetic, and creative problem-solvers. When developing service learning programs, reframing urban descriptors to focus on urban students' individual strengths can foster resilience and positive youth development (Heise, in press; Hutzel, 2007). Resilience, or the ability to cope in times of adversity, has been studied in social work (Greene, 2007; Greene, Taylor, Evans, & Smith, 2002), with families (Cowan, Cowan, & Shulz, 1996), with Holocaust survivors (Bar-Tur & Levy-Shiff, 1993; Greene, 2002), and with incarcerated youth (Cooper, 2003). However, resilience theory is relatively new to the field of art education.

In our program, we aimed to prepare teachers for success in an urban environment by constructing a curriculum that addressed elements of resilience within asset-based, mutually beneficial service learning opportunities. Asset-based community art education within the framework of resilience theory may inform art teacher preparation while empowering teachers and students to become change agents in their community (Heise, in press; Hutzel, 2007). Resilience theory in art education recognizes and celebrates individual and collective assets and uses strengths as a source of ideation. It builds on protective factors, such as flexibility and fluency, and resourcefulness in a nurturing environment. It encourages students to focus on aspirations and uses art to create a vision for the future (Heise, in press). Instead of being passive recipients of schools and society, urban youth become active participants in a democracy.

OUR NEIGHBORHOOD PROGRAM

The Community Arts Academy was a partnership between the art education program at the University of Memphis, the Davis Community Center, the University Neighborhood District Corporation, and Memphis Parks and Recreation. The academy took place weekly after school at a community center located at the heart of the University District, an area approximately half a mile from the university. Despite its name and its proximity to the university, most of our art education students had little knowledge of the neighborhood at the beginning of the program.

Most participating youth attended public middle schools in the neighborhood. This densely populated area consists largely of African Americans, with a growing Hispanic population (*38111 Zip Code Detailed Profile, n.d.*). The surrounding schools have between 90% and 100% students qualifying for free or reduced price lunch and a graduation rate of approximately 65% (School Diggers, 2010). Demographics also include a high infant mortality rate (Brooks et al., 2006; *38111 Zip Code Detailed Profile*, n.d.). Some community organizations are trying to improve the perceptions of this area. The University Neighborhood District Corporation (UNDC) is a nonprofit created to represent the mutual interests of the neighborhood groups in the University District, including the university, businesses, and residents (UNDC, 2009).

The many assets of the University District include a variety of housing options, including single-family homes and apartment complexes. In addition, there are numerous places of worship, small businesses, family-owned restaurants, and coffee shops. The community center has a gym, playground, and meeting spaces that are used by residents throughout the year. On some nights, the center is open late and members of the community gather to play basketball and table tennis. The center was also the site for an outdoor mural project done in conjunction with the city, two local universities, community center representatives, and students. A major asset of the neighborhood is the sense of community shared by its residents. Many of the families lived and grew up in this multi-age, multigenerational neighborhood and expressed pride in their community. Our program had strong support and parental involvement.

OUR CURRICULUM AND PLAYFUL APPROACH TO INSTRUCTION

We used a collaborative model to facilitate the design, implementation, and evaluation of art for urban youth. Our interdisciplinary curriculum focused on empowering participants by exploring art for social justice using a strengths-based philosophy of art education. Based on academic standards, each lesson also included artworks from at least three different cultures. Additionally, each lesson had to connect learning to young people's lives to enhance meaningful learning. Some lessons focused on making art that helps to promote awareness of the issues of human rights, such as the right to an education, the right to work, freedom from discrimination, and equality. The curriculum was guided by essential questions such as "What are human rights and why are they important to me?" and "How can I use the arts to increase awareness of human rights issues?" Using a resilience framework, students were guided to focus on possibilities for positive change.

University students embraced a pedagogy of play to engage participating youth and maintain classroom management. In this out-of-school setting, we used positive reinforcement and proximity rather than punitive measures to maintain a positive atmosphere. Instructional play differs from recreational play in that the activities are guided by learning objectives (Pitri, 2001). Games, simulations, and small- and large-group inquiry activities created enjoyable experiences while promoting learning. For example, one lesson used a game with balloons that were popped as a metaphor for bursting negative stereotypes. Others used role-play to engage youth and foster understanding and empathy. Engaging youth in enjoyable activities prevented disruptions. Teachers worked in teams to teach the curriculum, sitting with participating youth and creating with them. Verbal praise was utilized in recognizing success, focusing on the process as well as the product. We complimented effort, persistence, creativity, and resourcefulness, as well as composition and technique. We encouraged fluency and flexibility in the creative process. The implementation was relaxed and encouraged risk-taking in a nurturing environment.

LESSONS LEARNED THROUGH SERVICE IN COMMUNITY

Self-pity, exhaustion, and defeat described 1st-year teacher Jillian when she entered the licensure program at the University of Memphis as a graduate student. Hired on an alternate license in an urban school, Jillian felt she was at a disadvantage since she did not have the opportunity to student-teach prior to being hired. Though she loved her middle school students, Jillian complained that she often felt she spent too many days in survival mode. As classroom chaos resulted, with some days ending in tears, she had started to question her career choice. She attributed her stress to the particular school population where she taught. If she only had the privilege of teaching in a *better* neighborhood, she thought, her job would be easier.

Although Jillian was a graduate student who was already working in the field, her sentiments mirror those of many pre-service teachers who long to get a job in one of the "good schools." Kendal is an example of a typical undergraduate in the art education program at the University of Memphis. She was enthusiastic and eager to begin her teaching career; however, she hoped she would land a job in "a good school" with available resources, parental support, and students who are well behaved. Statements like these reveal that Kendal and her classmates assume that students in urban settings will be disengaged and unruly and that their parents would not care about their education. But Kendal did not recognize this at first. Like many undergraduates in urban art education programs, Kendal had limited interaction with middle school students and no experience teaching art in an urban environment prior to her participation in the Community Arts Academy.

It was this inexperience and apprehension about teaching in urban areas that motivated the art education faculty at the University of Memphis to design a course that provided professional development in urban education. We have chosen to focus on Jillian and Kendal as a narrative strategy to make personal the stories that seem to be repeated among our students from year to year. Their stories reveal lessons that were learned as they worked side by side with each other, with faculty members, and with youth and parents from the community. Experience developing community-based, culturally relevant curriculum, reciprocal mentoring, and relationship-building with members of the community emerged as important factors in their development. Critical reflection along the way helped Jillian and Kendal recognize assumptions and biases that could stand in the way of success in urban art teaching.

COMMUNITY-BASED CURRICULUM AND INSTRUCTION

As a result of participating in the Community Arts Academy, Kendal and Jillian reported that their confidence in their ability to teach in urban areas increased. Both cited the program's approach to curriculum as a factor that helped them gain confidence. Like all University of Memphis art education majors who were enrolled in graduate and undergraduate art education classes, Jillian and Kendal designed, implemented, and evaluated art lessons for youth ages 9–13 at the Academy while they learned about the community. University students realized that art can teach young people and their teachers how to be active in their community. Participating youth revealed increased awareness of social issues through art, and eagerness to "make a difference" (personal communication). By being immersed in the community, teachers and teacher candidates learned about cultural context and felt better prepared to facilitate meaningful teaching and learning.

As they developed collaborative curricula, Jillian, Kendal, and all of our students came to know people from the University District and learned about the many assets present in the neighborhood. Rather than seeing the neighborhood from the point of view of its deficits, as they had prior to their participation in the Community Arts Academy, the students learned to incorporate community assets into the curriculum in meaningful ways. In addition to collaborative curriculum-building, students also learned how art education can address social responsibility and social inequality. Instead of using art simply to illustrate principles and elements of design, they learned that it can be powerful in encouraging people to be empathetic, in seeing things from another perspective, and for communicating what we value. This illuminates the importance of creating curriculum within a framework of resilience theory as it relates to service learning for authentic experiences in teacher education and professional development.

The Community Arts Academy was developed to increase teacher confidence and competence in teaching diverse populations. Our experiences to date have been richly rewarding. This community collaboration, with its emphasis on teaching art and conducting research in urban areas, has been extremely beneficial to us as teacher educators. Our collaborative program prepared teachers for success in urban settings by enabling and encouraging them to:

- Create authentic teaching and learning experiences in urban environments for undergraduate and graduate students by reaching out to community members.
- Clearly communicate the expectations and roles of all involved in the community arts partnership.
- Develop a strengths-based curriculum: Consider a thematic curriculum that links learning to urban students' lives. Use individual and collective assets as a source of ideation for art making. Articulate positive characteristics in students, such as successful problem-solving, persistence, creativity, and resourcefulness.
- Use instructional play to engage students. Instructional play can increase enjoyment of the lessons and can be beneficial for both formal and informal learning environments. Use positive reinforcement for behavior management. Set high expectations for student learning and behavior and provide a safe learning environment that encourages alternative perspectives. Create a culture of success by setting clear guidelines and using praise to encourage responsible behavior.

- Be sensitive to strengths, challenges, and individuality of youth. Instead of stereotyping urban youth, spend time listening and getting to know them. Create responsive instructional materials and strategies that address different learning styles and possible language differences. Be flexible and adjust if necessary. Encourage them to take risks within a supportive environment.
- Critically reflect on teaching practices. Critically reflective practitioners question, redefine, and energize the field.
- Disseminate successes through exhibitions and by sharing at professional conferences. Consider sharing your story with other teachers by submitting a paper to a professional journal.

RECIPROCAL MENTORING

While they worked in the community with neighborhood residents, Jillian and Kendal reported that they also benefited from working with each other and with faculty members in the program. Indeed, a benefit that was mentioned by many students was the reciprocal mentoring that took place throughout the course. Reciprocal mentoring occurs when the roles of teacher and learner are alternated (Armon, Uhrmacher, & Ortega, 2009; Boyer, Maney, Kamler, & Comber, 2004). In this setting, undergraduates learned from peer mentors who were graduate students and 1st-year teachers. This often occurred through one-on-one informal talks that were made possible by the format of the program. These talks included both positive and negative teaching experiences. Through these talks, Kendal voiced that she "learned firsthand that teaching in an urban area can be very challenging; however, the rewards are worth the effort" (interview).

Graduate students also learned from co-teaching with undergraduates. Jillian stated that collaborating with undergraduates reminded her to be grateful for her teaching position. She considered their enthusiasm and high energy to be evidence of upcoming professionals who would love to have her job. In addition, graduate students mentored one another, using this as an opportunity to engage in formal and informal dialogue, to examine and analyze pedagogy of community-based programs and classroom experiences. It was common to hear them share challenges and insights from their recent experiences in school classrooms.

Seeing others teach and hearing how they talked to the students gave Jillian new ideas that she took back and implemented in her own classroom. As the end of the program neared, Jillian shared her disappointment: "I will miss [this]! We no longer have art teacher meetings in our district, and that makes me sad. What happens to art teachers doesn't happen to classroom teachers. Core teachers don't really understand our challenges. It has been so good to hear what is happening at other schools, and how other art teachers handle the challenges of teaching and discipline" (personal interview). The community of teachers created through the Community Arts Academy can be an ongoing source of support for the pre-service and in-service teachers who took part in it.

University students also reported the value of mentoring by university faculty. Submitting their lesson plans to university professors prior to teaching allowed them an opportunity to gain valuable feedback and critical reflection, and make necessary revisions. University professors worked side by side with undergraduates and graduate students in planning and implementing the program. This allowed them to see the professors as colleagues whose experience and understanding of the challenges faced by teachers in urban schools could be helpful to them.

BUILDING EMPATHY THROUGH PLAYFULNESS AND CRITICAL REFLECTION

Most importantly, college students and faculty learned from participating youth. They learned to listen more and talk less, and in the process learned more about the context of the children's lives. Unlike a traditional art classroom where the teacher often stands and teaches children who are seated at desks, these co-instructors sat among the children, facilitating informal dialogue in this co-learning environment. Our university students shared their appreciation for youths' attitudes toward learning new things. Even after being in school all day, many students wanted to learn about artists and participate in art activities. The critical reflection that was built into our process caused both undergraduate and graduate students to uncover their own assumptions about urban youth.

Additionally, instructional play as a pedagogical strategy helped students feel more positive about discipline and about students they had assumed would be unruly. Jeffers (2005) highlights the importance of empathy in education for helping build connections. Our playful approach to instruction helped build a capacity for empathy. By focusing on her students' strengths and approaching instruction in a playful way, Jillian noted that classroom management was easier than it had been for her in the past. Critical reflection helped Jillian, Kendal, and others see that the assumptions they had held about urban youth were erroneous and harmful. Their experiences in service to the community proved these assumptions to be untrue and counterproductive.

Consistent with what Hubbard (2009) found, teachers benefited from being immersed in another culture because it encouraged "examination of cultural assumptions and prejudices" (p. 41). Prior to implementation, Jillian felt that her challenges in the classroom were due to her specific student population. After experiencing professional growth in the program, she said, "I now know that kids are kids. They respond to how you teach. I learned how to communicate with them and not be afraid to enjoy them" (interview). Through the Community Arts Academy, both pre-service and in-service teachers grew by opening their minds to the lessons urban youth can teach. For both Jillian and Kendal, the program resulted in increased confidence and competence. Concerns about safety diminished as they interacted with participating youth. Prior to the program, they expressed concern about their ability to teach diverse student populations and apprehension about teaching in urban areas. As a result of participating in the program, they reported a renewed sense of purpose and enthusiasm for teaching diverse student populations. They felt that they now had something to offer urban students. Near the end of the program, Kendal announced her preference for teaching in an urban school, where she now felt she could make a difference in the lives of urban youth. Earlier, she had been reluctant to apply for a teaching position in an urban school district, yet after experiencing success with this community art program she enthusiastically awaited a response from her recent employment application.

NOTE

1. Jillian and Kendal are pseudonyms for composite representatives of undergraduate and graduate students with whom we worked in the Community Arts Academy. At the request of the editor, we employ a composite strategy to allow for a more compelling narrative flow in our chapter.

REFERENCES

Armon, J., Uhrmacher, P. B., & Ortega, T. (2009). The significance of self-portraits: Making connections through monotype prints in *letras y arte*. *Art Education, 62*(6), 12–18.

Bar-Tur, L., & Levy-Shiff, R. (1993). Holocaust review and bearing witness as a coping mechanism of an elderly Holocaust survivor. *Clinical Gerontologist, 14*(3), 5–16.

Boyer, I., Maney, B., Kamler, B., & Comber, B. (2004). Reciprocal mentoring across generations: Sustaining professional development for English teachers. *English Teaching: Practice and Critique, 3*(2), 139–150.

Brendtro, L. K., Ness, A. E., & Mitchell, M. (2005). *No disposable kids*. Bloomington, IN: National Education Service.

Cooper, N. (2003). *Resiliency development of incarcerated youth through outcome based recreation experiences* (Unpublished doctoral dissertation). Clemson University.

Cowan, P. A., Cowan, C. P., & Shulz, M. S. (1996). Thinking about risk and families. In M. Hetherington & E. A. Blechman (Eds.), *Stress, coping, and resilience in children and families* (pp. 1–38). Mahwah, NJ: Erlbaum.

Greene, R. R. (2002). Holocaust survivors: A study in resilience. *Journal of Gerontological Social Work, 37*, 3–18.

Greene, R. R. (2007). *Social work practice: A risk and resilience perspective*. Monterey, CA: Brooks/Cole.

Greene, R. R., Taylor, N., Evans, M., & Smith, L. A. (2002). Raising children in an oppressive environment. In Roberta R. Greene (Ed.), *Social work practice: A risk and resilience perspective* (pp. 241–276). Monterey, CA: Brooks/Cole.

Harper, N. R. (2008). Influencing K12 art programs. *Art Education, 61*(4), 47–50.

Heise, D. (in press). *Fostering resiliency through the arts.* In K. Tavin & C. B. Morris (Eds.), *Stand up for a change: Voices of arts educators.* Reston, VA: National Art Education Association.

Heise, D., & MacGillivray, L. (2010). *Analysis of an art and literacy program for children in a homeless shelter.* Paper presented at the National Art Education Convention, Baltimore.

Hutzel, K. (2007). Reconstructing a community, reclaiming a playground: A participatory action research study. *Studies in Art Education, 48*(3), 299–315.

Jacob, B. A. (2007). The challenges of staffing urban schools with effective teachers. *The Future of Children, 17*(1), 129–153.

Jeffers, C. (2005). *Spheres of possibility: Linking service-learning with the visual arts.* Reston, VA: National Art Education Association.

Payne, D. (2000). *Evaluating service-learning activities and programs.* Lanham, MD: Scarecrow.

Pearson, N. (1999). Social action as collaborative transformation. *Women's Studies Quarterly, 27*(3), 98–113.

Pitri, E. (2001). The role of artistic play in problem solving. *Art Education, 54*(3), 46–51.

Quinn, T., & Kahne, J. (2001). Wide awake to the world: The arts and urban schools. *Conflicts and contributions of an after-school program, 31*(1), 11–32.

School Diggers. (2010). *School summary.* Retrieved from http://www.schooldiggers.com. html.

Taylor, P. G. (2002). Service-learning as postmodern art and pedagogy. *Studies in Art Education, 43*(2), 124–140.

38111 Zip Code detailed profile. (n.d.). Retrieved from http://www.city-data.com/zips/38111. html.

Tredway, L. (1999). The art of juggling: Preparing preservice teachers for urban schools. *The Journal of Negro Education, 68*(3), 382–396.

UNDC (University Neighborhood District Corporation). (2009). *University District Comprehensive Plan.* Retrieved from http://www.memphisundc.com/documents.cfm.

7

Community Curriculum Matters

OLIVIA GUDE AND KIM COSIER

> Our goal is to create a beloved community and this will require a qualitative
> change in our souls as well as a quantitative change in our lives.
> —Martin Luther King Jr., *Testament of Hope*

When I invited Olivia to be part of this book project, she was concerned about
writing something that reified fixed definitions of "urban art education" as some-
how different from "normal" art education. As we discussed the potential of the
chapter, she said she felt the best way to talk about these issues was through a
dialogue format, which would represent our attempts to grapple with how various forms and uses of language shift perceptions of "the problem" and of how one
might create experiences for students and student teachers.

Toward that end, she invited me to stay for a weekend at her amazing artwork
of a home in Chicago to talk about teacher education and urban art education. We
discovered that we share an approach to urban art education that sees teachers
as cultural workers who can derive great benefit from seeing themselves as part
of the complex web of the urban community. It was an incredibly fun and ener-
gizing weekend, but the hard work was yet to come. This chapter is the result of
Olivia's transcription and condensation of digital recordings of a weekend's worth
of words. I had the relatively easy task of further refining and focusing our discussion and then sending it back to her for final revisions, which resulted in the form
you will read here. I am thankful to Olivia Gude for her good humor, thoughtful-
ness, hard work, and insight. We not only crafted a contribution to this book, but
we became good friends along the way.

Our discussions were intense and wide-ranging. However, out of 20,000 transcribed words, there emerged topics that we believe could be useful and challenging to people structuring urban art teacher education programs as well as students
who are interested in urban issues. We have distilled our dialogue into the following themes: thinking of the city as a rich resource and urban students as part of a
complex community; constructing an asset-based approach to urban art teacher
education that makes it possible for pre-service teachers to understand and honor

the richness of community; and the importance of creating an art education curriculum that blends theory and practice so that teachers as cultural workers can connect who we teach with what we teach. We hope you find our discussion challenging and useful.

THE CITY AS COLLAGE

OG: So, Kim, when I picked you up late last night you had a great Nighthawk's story (a "Nighthawk's story" refers to Edward Hopper's 1942 painting of people in a downtown diner late at night) to tell about an interesting "philosophical character" you encountered over a cup of coffee while waiting for me at a train station in downtown Chicago. This suggests an important theme that underlies our work as urban art educators—despite the many problems residents face, the city is also a place of surprise and opportunity. Living in a city is living in an intricate and intensely saturated collage.

KC: I love those chance encounters. The layered richness of urban life is one of the things we wanted to focus on in this book. I invited you to be part of my section on teacher education because I saw some parallels in the work that you were doing with the Spiral Workshop at the University of Illinois at Chicago and our program at the University of Wisconsin–Milwaukee. I was really interested in finding out more about how you had developed a program that is similarly situated in an urban center. You suggested this dialogical format. I agree it allows us to express the core of what we want to share—two experienced urban art educators developing our work by talking about the successes and issues that we encounter.

OG: My first response when I heard that you were contributing to a book on urban art education was, "I wouldn't know what to say about *that*," because I honestly didn't think about what I was doing as *urban art education*. I think of my work as developing art education content and methods that make sense for the students who we teach. My first question in developing art education curriculum is not "What should we teach?" but "Who are we teaching?" and "What do *these* students need to know?"

KC: Right, and of course that holds true for both the pre-service art educators and the K–12 students with whom they will work. As teacher educators who work in urban settings, questions about who we are teaching and what they need to know have an urgency because the students in our university programs are often culturally very different from the children and youth they will be teaching in urban schools.

OG: When I'm talking to my students who are studying to be teachers, I remind them that it is important to think of the "kids" (our kindergarten through high school students) not as isolated individuals, but as members of complex communities. Our job is to become community cultural workers—bringing valuable skills and knowledge to the community as well as learning from the community. Our goal is to create dialogical, art-based interactions that generate fresh ways of seeing and experiencing.

I try to connect this understanding of our work to the experiences of my students—a high percentage of whom are first-generation college students. I'm also a first-generation college student and I can recall the anxiety of feeling that the process of becoming educated was also a process of disconnecting from my roots, from my family and my cultural origins. My interest now is in creating a style of education in art that broadens students' life experiences, giving them a wider range of career and cultural choices, while deepening their connections to communities of origin.

KC: Definitely, those connections, within and across cultures, are really important. Part of my job in working with college students who see themselves as the norm, meaning white, middle-class and "not urban," is to make their own lives unfamiliar to them. Students will say, "I don't have a culture; my background—that I'm German or whatever—doesn't matter to me." I have to find an entry point so they think about the cultural specificity that each brings to the table so that the urban kids aren't the only ones who are marked, raced people.

At UMW, almost all of my college students come from outside of the city. Students often come to our program claiming, "I don't see color; I just see kids." They've seen popular media depictions of teachers who swoop in and save poor kids of color. They are sincere in wanting to be of service, so one thing I have to get them to realize is that they are also gaining something by being in Milwaukee, that there are positive things in the city that didn't happen where they come from. In order to teach, they have to learn from the children, too. It's a conceptual shift. For me, these two sides of the same coin are at the core of urban teacher education.

URBAN STUDENTS HAVE A LOT
TO LEARN—AND A LOT TO TEACH

KC: Some college students from the suburbs or small towns come in with stereotypical ideas of who an urban student is. They're not prepared to see city kids as individuals who are, as you said, members of complex communities. When encouraged to develop similarly complex curriculum, the response is: "But these kids can't use scissors!" Our response to that is, "So teach them skills through ideas, not drills."

In Elementary Methods, for example, we built some curriculum around the idea of mapping. One project, the Map of My Heart, was borrowed from artist Sarah Fanelli. Each student used the map format to visualize what was near and dear to them. They used scissors and rulers and other tools, but the experience did not end there. Students learned about Fanelli, a contemporary Italian artist, and they engaged in visual representation of things that mattered to them personally. It was an example of a way that you can teach skills while also capitalizing on urban students' experiences and encouraging them to engage in and contribute conceptually rich ideas.

OG: I remember doing a collage-based mural at a very poor urban school. I was shocked that many of the high school kids really couldn't use scissors. I realized that they had not had the opportunity to use scissors in elementary school—either because there was no money for such equipment or because someone had determined that even as 3rd-graders they were too dangerous to be given sharp objects. This is a good example of how kids can be systematically deprived of opportunities to develop skills and knowledge.

I've been in high schools where the students are laboriously using rulers to draw boxes to make a painted value scale. When I ask the teacher why she doesn't give the kids a xeroxed grid (or better yet, let the students freely form the rectangles with their paintbrushes as they mix the values), the response is, "These kids need to practice using a ruler; *some* of them can't even read the fractions." Two comments—one, is it fair to make *all* the kids do tediously repetitive work when some *already* have this skill? Doesn't this guarantee that these kids will also be pushed into another "these kids can't" category because of wasted learning time? Two, if you do want to teach these kids to use a ruler, aren't there better, more interesting methods? For example, how about collaboratively creating a huge line mural based on a Sol LeWitt wall drawing instructions? [LeWitt, a conceptual artist, believed that a drawing was just a physical manifestation of an idea and could be done by anyone following and artist's instructions. Thus, he developed mathematically derived instructions for large-scale wall drawings.]

KC: Right, remediation and skill-building can't mean a dumbed-down curriculum. Students in urban public schools may come to us with deficits related to a host of economic and social barriers to "achievement," so our challenge becomes more interesting than it might be in well-funded suburban schools. Projects must teach skills *and* open up opportunities for exploration of ideas that are culturally relevant and interesting to urban kids.

CONNECTING ART PEDAGOGY TO COMMUNITY ASSETS

OG: It's important to understand urban communities within a community assets framework as opposed to a community deficits model. College students can be surprised by how, when prompted, urban kids can readily talk about what's good about their neighborhoods and cultural backgrounds—perhaps as opposed to things they don't like that they see in other settings and cultures. A strength that urban kids often bring to the table is the concept of "community."

Frequent references to *community* in contemporary times originate in communities of color, what Martin Luther King called "beloved community." Whatever problems are in a neighborhood because of poverty, racism, historical neglect, or because of poor choices that people in the community have sometimes made, connectedness is one of the community strengths. It's important that urban art teacher education introduces students to the rich cultures that have evolved in communities—the street mural movement, hip-hop, jazz, poetic and amusing vernacular language. What can movements such as the AfriCobra group in Chicago or Mujeres Muralistas in California tell us about the past and about possibilities in the future?

The curriculum industry of art education emphasizes formalist and technical art knowledge as well as the art history of canonical works. Diversity is used as spice for the main menu, not as a challenge to the basic recipe. Quality art curriculum must evolve out of specific contexts and histories, instead of importing and imposing supposedly neutral, universal aesthetic practices.

KC: Sometimes college students find it surprising that it's not enough just to rely on commercially produced curriculum materials and the art education they had in K–12 or in college. They'll make the "cultural capital" argument that kids need access to the greatest works to be truly educated. We try to shift their thinking from focusing on the canon to learning from the lives of the kids and, from there, to figure out ways to access and utilize various knowledge bases.

It's important to look to the visual culture of the community, as well as contemporary artists of color and a diversity of contemporary art practices as a model for the classroom. Coming to children with a focus on historical and contemporary local culture honors what they bring to you. It's a valid and important struggle to get our novice teachers to move out of their comfort zone, to relinquish the position of the all-knowing teacher and to get comfortable in unsafe intellectual space by looking and re-looking. They have an impulse to be in control, but culturally relevant teaching insists on relinquishing some control and being able to learn from the community.

OG: Yes, although I often talk to my young teachers, reinforced by reading Lisa Delpit's (1995) book, *Other People's Children*, about the necessity of having coherent, strong models of discipline within the classroom. Good discipline is defined not as having the control of lots of little rules that must be obeyed, but as kids wanting to cooperate and participate because the teacher is an authority figure who is committed to their total well-being and to teaching them things that will allow them to grow and prosper.

Any teacher should be knowledgeable about and should bring to the children the absolute best, most sophisticated thinking and art that people of the kids' racial and ethnic group are developing. When teaching in a Black community, I need to bring historical understanding of the evolution of African American aesthetics, of the African diaspora, of the interrelationships of history, culture, and art-making in the Black experience. Of course, it's also important that kids have the opportunity to experience and understand the complicated and sophisticated work of artists of all colors because if kids don't have that they are not prepared to be cosmopolitan citizens of the 21st century. However, developing keen awareness and a desire to know has to begin with interest in things that feel intimately related to oneself.

KC: Yes, making those intimate connections is the key to engagement, which usually makes irrelevant and unnecessary all the little rules teachers have an urge to impose on kids in urban schools. A curricular focus on the assets of a community may be more difficult at the outset than drawing from commercially available resources and from your own past education, but ultimately it is more rewarding for everyone involved. Of course, culturally relevant curriculum and instruction alone don't necessarily mean that teachers make important connections between the "whos" and the "whys" of urban art education—they need theory to do that.

INTERTWINING THEORY AND PRACTICE
IN URBAN ART TEACHER PREPARATION

OG: Yes, another thing our programs seem to have in common is an integration of theory and practice. Art teacher education programs have often asked young teachers to do in schools what they haven't done in the universities. The students take separate studio, art history, and education classes. Even within the art education program, study is often broken up into an art interpretation course, a history of art education course, a visual culture course, a course in studio methods, et cetera. The art education curriculum itself is organized in terms of the specialties of the professors! Then, young teachers are directed to envision an art education methodology that intertwines these subjects, that embodies the interpenetration of theory and art-making.

KC: The problem of practicing what we preach is a sticky one. At UMW our methods courses are 6-credit experiences that combine engagement in theories connected to critical pedagogy and critical race theory, feminist, queer, disability, and whiteness studies, and so on, with teaching in public schools. In this way, our students come to see that theory can help us explain the "whys" of urban education. Two professors teach in the classroom at the university in the mornings and then the group splits and we go out to two different schools in the afternoons. Our students can see that we are good teachers, that we can talk to kids and handle "situations" when they come up. This gives us a common set of experiences to use as examples when teaching pedagogical theory. I'm not sure if this methodology is more important because we are working in an urban setting, or if this is a good way of teaching no matter where you are.

OG: I think this methodology is important no matter where we are, but the crisis of education is more acute in urban settings. It's clear that the system is working for the status quo and not for these communities. It's a crisis of resources and of meaning. The kids don't believe that learning this curriculum, learning these elements and principles, will have a positive effect on their current or future lives. Can we invent templates of curricula in which kids learn art skills as they are investigating authentic cultural questions and making personally meaningful work? Can we develop curriculum in which traditional and contemporary art and methods of making are presented in contexts that emphasize how these are tools for pleasurable and effective contemporary living?

KC: I hope so! Investigating authentic cultural questions and making personally meaningful work is key. In our secondary methods course students collaboratively develop thematic curricula to teach in our partner schools, the teaching groups have to pitch their ideas to the public school students, and the kids get to choose which project they want to participate in.

OG: I like that the novice teachers have to sell their work to their students. I use as rubrics for my young teachers "Develop an art education practice that could survive without a compulsory attendance policy" and "Teach skills and ways of thinking and making that are so intrinsically interesting and useful the students will use them without being warned that there will be an assessment."

In Foundations of Art Education at UIC, we introduce the idea of dialogical pedagogy and identifying generative themes. We look at real-life examples of curriculum in which themes in kids' lives are the focus of art projects. The next semester our central practicum experience is Spiral Workshop, a Saturday art program for teens from throughout the Chicago area. Spiral is also a curriculum research laboratory. I meet with each group of novice teachers, planning theme-based curriculum during the week. We teach the teens on Saturday morning and then spend the afternoon reviewing each other's curricula. We collectively listen to the kids' emerging voices and consider what the next steps should be. At the end of the 9-week sequence, we hold a Spiral Show and Community Reception at which the kids, their families and friends, area teachers and others come together to see the results of this year's theme investigations into subjects such as "Bling," "Cute," "Disorder," "Apparitions," and "Liminality."

KC: I love the idea of a curriculum research laboratory. In support of the kind of practice we are talking about you've done a great job of sharing curriculum through your Spiral websites (spiral.aa.uic.edu and naea.digication. com/Spiral/Spiral_Workshop_Theme_Groups/). I think a strength our programs share is the deep engagement of the faculty members with the field experiences, taking theory and putting it into practice. If we're not there wrestling with the day-to-day issues of doing this sort of teaching, it's somewhat hypocritical to ask students of teaching to do so.

OG: As I sit in planning sessions with the teachers of a Spiral group, sometimes we are tearing our hairs out, trying to come up with a way to examine a theme that would "work," that will create compelling and exciting curriculum and art. Sometimes when my students get really frustrated I say to them, "This is objectively difficult. It's not difficult because you're slow, because I'm not a good professor, or because someone is slacking. It's really hard to imagine and to work ourselves into a new pedagogical space."

KC: Yes, it is difficult work, but by developing curriculum together we are modeling the sort of research and ideation, the curriculum and teaching practices, that we'd like the students to engage in. We struggle to find ways for all of our pre-service teachers to "get" this approach. The addition of Stewart and Walker's (2005) *Rethinking Curriculum in Art* has been helpful, with its focus on Big Ideas. But it still takes tenacity on our parts to enact this sort of teacher education.

OG: Though I understand the desire of some professors to engage in reconceptualizing art education without prescribing what should happen in classrooms, I'm also suspicious that this path is not likely to foster proactive, imaginative structures for creating personal and collective meaning. When I see an art education lecture illustrated with a few fabulous, idiosyncratic pieces that were made by an experienced high school senior in an AP class, I worry. It's not that it's not great to see students working independently in sophisticated ways, but how do we develop curriculum to get all students to that place?

It's worth mentioning that what allows us to do this careful, focused curriculum development with our students in school settings is that we make this work part of our research as professors. Given the value system of the university, one cannot put in this kind of time unless this work is also formulated as a research agenda.

THE IMPORTANCE OF *CREATING INVESTIGATIONS* AND MAKING MEANING THROUGH ART

OG: I'm hearing that in both of our programs initial art teacher education experiences include a lot of making because people can't teach things well that they haven't experienced themselves. Most of today's teacher candidates haven't experienced using art projects as a collective structure you can utilize to do authentic investigations of things that are important to you. I think of art projects as an art form. Artworks make meaning through the play of form and content.

When we make up a good art project, we've designed an open structure that other people can get inside to make meaning. As a community-based artist, I pay careful attention to the kinds of structures that need to be developed to investigate emerging generative themes.

In Spiral, we use the term "theme curriculum" to describe our curriculum style. I've tried to figure out the complexity of how we use the concept of themes. In some ways, it's a big idea. But I find myself always talking about the importance of staying in the images, staying in particulars, staying in messy, metaphoric spaces. It's unlikely that we would do a theme called "Stop Bullying"; it's too literal. We have done a theme group called "Conflict & Resolution: Pencils & Pixels." We considered whether there is an intrinsic conflict between the hand-drawn and the digital at the same time we considered various social manifestations of conflict and resolution. We set up a material/formal and conceptual dichotomy. As those four terms in the title started to operate against and amongst each other, it created an investigation of areas of conflict and how the ways in which conflicts are framed and the individual terms are valued affects the possibility of resolution.

KC: Making the technical aspects of the project communicate with the big idea that they are using can be tricky for new teachers. They'll come up with a theme such as "conflict" and they end up doing some completely unrelated art-making process. They've got a nifty-looking project going on over here, but it doesn't relate to the content over there.

OG: My archetypal example of a form/content misfit is trying to do a linoleum block print about memory. Here's a medium in which it is difficult to create fine detail, that has to be preconceived, abstracted to high contrast, flipped into a mirror image, and then laboriously carved and printed. It's not that I'm against block printing, but when you are trying to do certain kinds of content investigations, it's not a good fit. Memory is elusive, shifting, and uncertain. What media might be used for such a subject?

KC: I wrote curriculum for 4th-graders in which the students made small, snapshot-sized drawings of objects that signified strong memories of early childhood. We looked at the work of Hollis Sigler and Doris Salcedo to free them from the constraints of the literal and to think about how objects can stand in for people.

OG: That's a good example of expanding a teacher's toolkit for creating investigations and making meaning. How does the art-making not just illustrate but cultivate conceptual awareness or shift affective states? Early in the Foundations course, we do a project called "Space and Place" in which students use cut paper collage as the medium for recollecting memories of a significant place in childhood. It's an anti-linear-perspective project, created in colored paper collage so that planes can shift and details can be gradually layered onto the image. We might make use of diagonal or converging lines to create the illusion of depth on the flat plane, but eschew the metaphorical implications of one-point perspective. What does it mean to think that there is a single correct way to look at or remembering something?

In this course, we consider a range of aesthetic practices, including expressionism, deconstruction, and appropriation/reclamation. Looking at a wide range of artists whose work can be loosely classified as expressionistic, we ask, what does it mean to make things through tracking one's own bodily sensations? What does it mean to depict things in which one consciously interweaves one's own subjectivity with representations of the world? Are expressionist aesthetic practices a tool that students can use to make contemporary meaning?

It's important to rethink the meta-narratives of art history. A standard understanding of modernism in the visual arts is that it was increasingly focused on abstraction, form, and medium. However, that reading of art history requires that we leave out important figures—for example, Jacob Lawrence's work (like the cubists) makes use of African-inspired form, but for Lawrence this wasn't just a formal appropriation, it's a reclamation of cultural and political signifiers. Understanding this conceptual and aesthetic shift gives pre-service teachers tools to see art and aesthetics as the source material for creating a sense of self. It builds in them the capacity to understand contemporary African American artists such as Michael Ray Charles, Mark Bradford, or Lorna Simpson who explore personal and social implications of living in a culture imbued with the legacy and the actuality of racial coding.

Think about the modernism of the Mexican mural movement. Artists like Siqueros, Rivera, and Orozco were very aware of the stylistic experimentation going on in Europe, but rather than make art only for individual collectors, they focused on making a public art for La Raza, the new people of Mexico. This way of thinking is not only about overtly political works—it recognizes that all artists take where they come from and think about how to use this to make something new. That's a great image for students in formulating how to think of themselves as citizens of the world.

KC: The self is always moving and changing. How can art-making and other experiences in schools get children to a place where they see themselves as determined by circumstances and capable of self-determination? If you don't really examine what's happening now, you can't imagine a different future. We're trying to get the college students to practice art-making and curriculum development that questions what seems given and natural in order to reveal that "normal" is a social construction that maintains oppression. The marginalization of art in urban schools is one result, which often strikes a chord with our students.

OG: Most art teachers today express belief in the value of using art for telling personal stories, documenting community histories, honoring and extending local cultural traditions, and investigating how dominant media can create beliefs that undermine a kid's sense of possibility and power. These are values of the community arts movement. These values are not always manifested in the current school arts curriculum, but that's a gap of practice, not of belief. It's important that projects such as this book share clear and specific pictures of exemplary community art practices in school and other settings. A transformation of art education is happening, and it's happening at a grass-roots level. It's not going to happen because the standards are changed; the standards are going to change when there are many vivid examples of engaged, relevant art education practices.

I see this chapter as representing (in a highly edited form, of course) the dialogical nature of the encounter of art educators and communities. A dialogical educator comes to the teaching situation with humility, without the assumption that he/she already knows what categories must be addressed, what questions must be answered. One listens and forms tentative formulations without the overbearing assumption that one's role is to provide the outline or the summation for everyone involved.

KC: This back-and-forth kind of teaching and learning is key to crafting a shared power and a shared vision. With our minds open to learning in the community—in dialogue with others as we have here—we, and our students, can become part of the complex cultural collage of the city.

REFERENCES

Delpit, L. (1995). *Other people's children: Cultural conflict in the classroom.* New York: New Press.

King, M. L. (1986). *Testament of hope: The essential writings and speeches of Martin Luther King* (J. M. Washington, Ed.). New York: HarperCollins.

Stewart, M., & Walker, S. (2005). *Rethinking curriculum in art.* Worcester, MA: Davis Publications.

Part III

Engaging Pedagogy: Curriculum and Methodologies for the City

KAREN HUTZEL AND SHARIF BEY

This free space is a possible world that breaks down social barriers and allows young people to name themselves, envision alternative realities, and engage in remaking their worlds.
—Debra Holloway and Beth Krensky,
"Introduction: The Arts, Urban Education, and Social Change"

Narrative by Sharif Bey, co-author of this part introduction: *In 1947 my father and his family moved to Beltzhoover, a diverse and self-sustaining community on the Southside of Pittsburgh. As a young man he patronized countless local businesses blocks away from his home (N. Bey, personal communication, June 9, 2010). By the 1970s, Beltzhoover had transformed into a still thriving predominantly African American neighborhood, although many of the aforementioned businesses closed as White families and business owners moved away. The vacant commercial buildings and storefronts compelled my brother and me to ask questions about our neighborhood history. These queries prompted our elders to share stories about Beltzhoover in the 1950s. Their stories gave meaning to these physical structures. Naturally, we paralleled their tales to our relationship to the neighborhood.*

In the 1980s, Beltzhoover still boasted of one of the best elementary schools in the city and annually put on an astonishing community day parade where local business owners participated alongside community organizations, firemen, police officers, clowns, children, and Clydesdale horses. In this urban landscape, we seldom found boredom. Unbeknownst to us, the steel mills were shutting down and unemployment, alcoholism, drugs, and violence were beginning to take hold of our neighborhood. But thanks to youth programs, recreational facilities, and inspiring stories, there was never a dull moment.

As a young boy, I wandered beyond my uncle's backyard to discover an auto mechanics garage in the alley behind his house. While I had experienced the interior of a mechanics shop before, there were several things that distinguished this one from the others. There were usually a few cars on jack stands in the large driveway outside of the main garage where John Taggart, the owner, worked. Taggart, who was a house painter by trade, was in his fifties and learned auto mechanics as a boy in rural Georgia. There in his alley, teenage boys worked on their own vehicles alongside him. Through Taggart's generosity, they had the benefit of his experience and the use of his state-of-the-art tools. At the time I wasn't so impressed by this, but hanging out in the back alley provided me with an opportunity to listen to older boys talk about sex and other teenage interests. After this discovery, I spent less time playing in my uncle's yard and more time listening at the fence or trying to get a glimpse of the covered racecar next to Taggart's workstation. I was enamored by the car's mystery. We never heard the rumble of the engine and Taggart always kept it covered, but the mystique of this vehicle and its giant bald racing tires left a lot for the imagination.

After a while I noticed that some of the posters, photos, and calendars that graced the walls of the shop included photographs of a younger John Taggart wearing a racing helmet and posing in various race cars. I was told that before my time, Taggart raced and sometimes cruised his race car down the street in the annual neighborhood community day parade. I spent a lot of time with Taggart in subsequent years, as I also made repairs of my own after purchasing my first used car.

In the past 50 years, Beltzhoover has lost more than two-thirds of its population. Like many urban communities, fleeting industry, crack trade, and associated violence have left our neighborhood in shambles. Most of the commercial property has been leveled. The vacant storefronts that sparked our imaginations in the 1980s are nonexistent; therefore, they no longer prompt the oral histories or sustain significant neighborhood memories. The children of Beltzhoover now dwell in a ruinous urban landscape. As elders pass and important structures are torn down, teachers face new challenges when attempting to locate neighborhood histories and assets to interpret and expand upon through meaning-making activities.

Bey's childhood experience in his community exemplifies many possibilities for education in the city that can engage children in examining their communities through art. Teachers and schools who value a dynamic and critical approach to student learning and an asset-based perspective about the students and their community suggest possibilities for art to engage children in seeking possibility in themselves and their cities, imagining hopeful futures and communities, and exploring urban visualities and realities. In this part the authors provide curricula and stories of urban art education pedagogies promoting social justice through art instruction both inside and outside the classroom.

Curriculum, what is taught in schools, reflects a society's values and can vary from school to school. In some schools, children are taught critical thinking and problem solving skills in preparation for future leadership. In other schools, children are taught basic reading, writing, and mathematics skills focused on test-taking, with strict behavioral implications. In this era of accountability through test-taking, school for many children has become irrelevant, disconnected, and often unbearable. School subjects and curricula that *enhance* educational experiences for children are often replaced when schools face pressure to prepare children to pass state tests. In a research study, Mishook and Kornhaber (2006) found that in schools serving economically disadvantaged students, arts education was used primarily to prepare students to take the exams. "Schools with high numbers of poor children face the twin dangers of low-quality arts education and teaching practices where test preparation and curricular narrowing are more likely to take place in response to the introduction of high-stakes testing" (Mishook & Kornhaber, 2006, p. 10). Many schools now promote memorization over problem-solving, critical thinking, and creative expression, which can prepare students to participate actively as engaged community members. As Ballengee-Morris and Stuhr (2001) concede, "We may have become bogged down in the teaching of school subjects or disciplines in a way that they are no longer connected to the students' lives" (p. 6). Many urban students, especially, are suffering the consequences of teaching methods that promote testing over innovation. The challenge to prepare students to do well on tests results in curriculum that emphasizes facts and figures over people and communities. This part, however, offers possibilities for engaging children in life-enhancing educational experiences in the city through community-based and local art, reasserting the inherent value in centering art and the city in school curriculum.

This part offers pedagogies of possibility through application of teaching through an asset-based foundation of art education. Building on the previous two parts, this final part suggests practical approaches and meaningful success stories of curriculum development and educational practices rooted in constructivist learning and cultural relevance, and considerate of local issues and concerns. Chapters highlight visual art and culture curricula and programs in schools that utilize student and community assets and resources while building on local cultural dynamics manifested through visual art.

In Chapter 8, I (co-author of this introduction, *Karen Hutzel*) suggest collaborative art-making through service learning as a method by which to value students' abilities and attributes while responding to local culture. In Chapter 9, *Kristien Zenkov* and *Kimberly Sheridan* share a photography approach as a method by which to highlight and represent children's voices and perceptions of their school lives while promoting literacy. In Chapter 10, *Mindi Rhoades* suggests the possibility for empowering marginalized youth, specifically LGBTQ youth, through video production and community education. *Carol Ng-He*, in Chapter 11, offers the relatively new Chicago Teen Museum as an example of possibility within urban schools through partnerships and teen involvement. In Chapter 12, *James H. Rolling Jr.* provides a pedagogy to engage elementary students in exploring and suggesting sacred spaces within their city landscapes. And in Chapter 13, *Melanie Buffington* and *Erin Waldner* suggest exploring, researching, and interpreting public art in the city while proposing new public art.

Each chapter has an accompanying unit plan overview (located in the Appendix) to assist educators in developing curriculum relevant to their school's city and local community. The unit plans are presented loosely to encourage educators to share the task of exploring and investigating the local in partnership with students, through a constructivist and asset-based approach to teaching and learning. Each city is different. Each community has its own treasures. Each student has ideas. And each school and teacher can engage children in connecting and honoring their local, personal, cultural, environmental, and physical assets through art.

REFERENCES

Ballengee-Morris, C., & Stuhr, P. (2001). Multicultural art and visual cultural education in a changing world. *Art Education, 34*(4), 6–13.

Holloway, D. L., & Krensky, B. (2001). Introduction: The arts, urban education, and social change. *Education and Urban Society, 33*(4), 354–365.

Mishook, J. J., & Kornhaber, M. L. (2006). Arts integration in an era of accountability. *Arts Education Policy Review, 107*(4), 3–11.

8

A Possibility of Togetherness

Collaborative Art Learning for Urban Education

KAREN HUTZEL

The key to meaning making, though, lies in our ability to make connections—
by understanding relationships between one thing and the other and between
one person and another.
                                        —Tom Anderson and Melody Milbrandt, *Art for Life*

It has become evident that urban schools are struggling. Teachers burn out quickly. Principals are under intense pressure. Students are facing extreme challenges. The problems of urban schools are well known, but solutions tend to focus heavily on students' problems. In contrast, the possibility of collaboration through art and service learning (collaborative art learning) represents a pedagogy building on student attributes and school and community assets. This chapter offers strategies and ideas for creating engaging opportunities for students to connect with their local community and one another through collaboration and art-making. Collaborative art learning can provide substantial opportunities for enhancing learning in urban settings where schools are often culturally diverse, students sometimes face daily life challenges, and community and school environments have significant untapped histories. Collaborative art learning as a teaching approach can recognize student assets, celebrate local culture, and provide social and emotional learning (Russell & Hutzel, 2007) through the creation of an exciting, inquiry-based learning atmosphere.

DIVERSE SCHOOLS AND MULTICULTURAL POSSIBILITIES

Upon moving to Columbus, Ohio, my husband and I decided to enroll my step-daughter, then 3rd-grader Brianna, in the Columbus City Schools for the educational experience and personal enrichment of being in a diverse setting. We felt it was important for her, particularly as a biracial child, to be in an environment where her racial designation was not necessarily her school's main identifier of her. At her school in the Columbus City School district, there was a diverse mix of children who were labeled and identified as African American, White, multiracial, Latino, and Asian, including children identified with special needs and many who have tested as "gifted and talented." The socioeconomic status of the student population is predominately working and middle-class, with a high percentage of students qualifying for free and reduced price lunch. The teachers and staff seem to be a near-equal mix of White and African American. The school's diversity rests primarily on this ethnic diversity as a cultural indicator.

Conversations about diversity are abundant, but are foundationally intended to remind us to recognize and value our cultural differences. However, the testing and accountability movement has done the opposite, as it positions diversity as a challenge schools must deal with in order to achieve on standardized tests. Yet, as Ballengee-Morris and Stuhr assert, "it is important to understand culture and cultural diversity because culture provides beliefs, values, and patterns that give meaning and structure to life" (2001, p. 6). Referencing several educational scholars, Ballengee-Morris and Stuhr (2001) continued the argument for the integration of culture and cultural diversity in education, stating:

> It enables individuals within the multiple social groups of which they are a part to function effectively in their social and cultural environments, which are constantly changing. Education is part of cultural experience; therefore, it cannot be reduced to disciplinary parameters but should include issues of power, history, and self-identity. (p. 6)

Schools serving working- and middle-class urban populations are often places where various cultures come together, presenting unique possibilities for multicultural education through collaborative learning and community-building. The possibility of social reconstruction is suggested in multicultural learning theories (Sleeter & Grant, 1999), conceptually underscoring my proposal for collaborative art learning as an educational strategy.

RE-ENGAGING STUDENTS THROUGH COLLABORATIVE ART LEARNING

Recent challenges in education born out of strict testing requirements have disenfranchised, disengaged, and disconnected children from schools, suggesting a need to re-engage children in learning how to live in the 21st century. Many years ago, Davis (1993) analyzed and reported from the work of multiple researchers suggesting that collaborative learning *actively engages* students in the learning process (Beckman, 1990; Chickering & Gamson, 1991; Collier, 1980; Cooper & Associates, 1990; Goodsell, Maher, Tinto, & Associates, 1992; Johnson & Johnson,

1989; Johnson, Johnson, & Smith, 1991; Kohn, 1986; McKeachie, Pintrich, Lin, & Smith, 1986; Slavin, 1980, 1983; Whitman, 1988). Davis (1993) claimed that students learn more when working collaboratively, retain knowledge longer, and are more satisfied with their classes. Anderson and Milbrandt (2005) suggest art education focus on life-enhancing practices through inquiry-based curricular methods, suggesting collaboration as a particular avenue to reach students. Community murals are offered as an example of utilizing collaboration in promoting sense of community and place, offering an opportunity for urban kids to leave a positive mark on their community.

Service learning is a recent and popular methodology to collaborative learning focused on civic engagement as a curricular approach to teaching subject matter. There are many ways to implement service learning, and a focus on filling needs often underscores this teaching methodology. However, calls for reciprocity in service learning activities have highlighted an inherent problem with this needs-based approach in that participants in service learning partnerships are often unrecognized for their attributes and possibilities, reinforcing the inequitable social systems that have maintained their oppressed status. Critical thinking, social justice, and the potential to create change are more likely outcomes when recognizing the abilities each participant brings to the collaboration. In a multicultural approach to collaboration and service learning, "teachers stress the unique contributions of individuals drawn from diverse groups" (Ballengee-Morris & Stuhr, 2001, p. 9). An asset-based approach furthers the possibility of recognizing and building on students' abilities as opposed to their problems.

Art-based collaboration and service learning have become more prevalent in recent years. Artists work in collaboration with each other and with community members in many ways. Their methods of collaborative art-making provide educators with possibilities for curriculum that engages students and community members in meaningful ways. Olivia Gude, for instance, has collaboratively constructed murals across Chicago, working with various groups of children and adults to build on local assets. The group Improv Everywhere, described by Richardson (2008), regularly involves hundreds of individuals in making social statements through what might be described as performance art. Arynn McCandless, an artist and educator in Cincinnati, Ohio, described her collaborative processes, varying from her role as a facilitator of children envisioning their own work (individual or in collaboration with one another) to a role as lead artist, guiding children toward a particular artistic goal with their ideas informing the concepts imbedded in the final piece (personal communication, November 10, 2008). Cooper and Sjostrom (2006) described their process of facilitating collaborative art experiences with students beginning with simple individual drawings. With a larger, collaborative art piece in mind, Cooper engaged his students in individual art-making activities then connected together to create a final artwork representative of multiple voices. "Service-learning and the arts share an approach to education that promotes authentic, active, community-connected learning. Both provide opportunities to focus on competencies, such as teamwork and problem-solving skills, and both share core values" (Jobs for the Future, quoted in Cho, 2006, p. 2).

BEGINNING WITH COMMUNITY:
MODELS OF COLLABORATIVE ART LEARNING

The local context is central to collaborative art learning, suggested by Anderson and Milbrandt (2005) to rest on sense of self, sense of place, and sense of community. Common factors in collaborative art learning practices include: (1) appreciation for assets each participant brings to the team, (2) development of group meaning around a community issue, (3) focus on the local community culture, and (4) strategies toward a common goal and tangible product. In each of the following examples, these factors seem relevant to the success for student learning, beginning with an environmentally conscious student service learning project in the Florida Keys and ending with an imaginative, place-based art teacher in a low-income school east of Columbus, Ohio. While there is a common environmental theme to these examples, localness is emphasized and underscores the value to the students and community.

Celebrating the Environment through Art and Design

At Coral Shores High School in the Upper Keys of Florida, a service learning course encouraged students to develop and lead their own service learning projects. One such project provided an opportunity for a particular student to focus her efforts on developing a week full of Earth Day activities for the community, in which the environment was profoundly important. This student, however, faced some challenges in school and wasn't sure of her future. She wasn't confident in her abilities to create her own service learning project, but had an idea for the upcoming Earth Day celebration. She gathered a small team of her peers from her service learning class to brainstorm activities to celebrate the Earth. They then enlisted the help of their teachers.

As a group, the students and teachers developed activities for the Earth Week celebration, divvying up responsibilities and tasks. At the beginning of the week, the entry hallway of the school was decorated as an underwater environment, which created an atmosphere of peace and serenity. Teachers commented on how well behaved students were in the hallway during the week, as the faint glow of the lights, which were covered in blue and green, appealed to students and faculty. The week also included a door-decorating contest, in which homerooms were charged with decorating the classroom doors with found objects to represent "Reduce, Reuse, and Recycle." Many students were found digging through recycling bins throughout the school and searching for items to use in their designs. Almost every classroom in the school participated in the contest, displaying creativity and excitement in their designs. The student who initiated the activity spoke for the first time over the intercom and revealed leadership qualities she seemed uncertain of at the beginning of the project.

A Whale, a Mural, a Song, and a Changed Place

Mary Sheridan, an elementary art teacher, had found herself surrounded by high school students recently at the end of the school day. As Mary shared stories of these particular teenagers when they were in her elementary school art classes, occasionally holding back tears, I recognized just why so many of her former students came back to see her. She had instilled in them a sense of place based on the impacts they made on the school. According to Mary, a quiet girl who was standing at the side of the group of animated high school students looked up to the groups and said, "I got to paint a mural while I was here." Mary asked what her name was. "Anastasia," the girl said to her. Mary gave her a hug and said, "I was harder on you than I've ever been in my career."

Mary said her students, whose school was moved to a new building with new children in 1996, many transient and most lower-income, suffered from a disconnection from their environment. The most challenging students were often sent to her to participate in collaborative art programs and Anastasia, whose father had just gotten out of jail and whose behavior had become unmanageable by other teachers in the school, came to Mary as a last resort. While Anastasia was suspended, Mary went to her in an effort to break through to her. Mary said to her, "I am going to give you an opportunity to be part of a team, you are going to have to bring it. You can't just come and get out of class. You're going to have to keep up with your classwork. You're going to have to quit lying and stealing and all this other stuff. Is this something you want to do?" Remembering the tears streaming down the young girl's cheeks, Mary recalled how saddened she was to be so harsh, knowing this young girl needed clear boundaries. Anastasia showed up the next day with a folder full of sketches. Every day after that she came ready to work. As a teenager, Anastasia looked to Mary and responded to her comment, "Mrs. Sheridan, I haven't been in trouble since then."

Mary walked me around the school that day, showing me a double-sided quilt with water imagery on one side and greenery on the other, the students having participated in multiple environmental education activities that contributed to its conception. She described the multiple visiting artists she had brought to the school and the various local and environmental groups she involved in her lessons. Mary said she focuses her curriculum on community issues to make it relevant to the students' lives, with the idea of "changing places" at the heart of the integrated arts curriculum. It started with the move to the new school, and took on many forms through the next 12 years, emphasizing ongoing projects that evolved over time. She recognized that her new school location included a more transient population seemingly disconnected from their community and children who didn't have the land in which to wander and explore. This understanding provided the foundation of her teaching approach, which emphasized place. Ultimately, she wanted to realize the school grounds as the "backyard for the kids" in their community.

Mary showed me a pond the students had created outside the back door of her art classroom. It started with a flock of ducks continually coming to the back door of the classroom, which instilled a sense of curiosity in the kids. Mary revealed to me that she had been putting food outside the door to draw them in, and then used their presence to consider their needs (a pond), their response to noises in the school (a project on sound), and their young ducklings (quiet engagement with nature). These activities have taken place over many years, challenging traditional notions of curriculum in an ongoing and organic nature.

Imagination based on reality seems inherent in everything Mary includes in her curriculum. A lesson on sound eventually involved the students in working collaboratively with a group in Alaska, as they considered how sound impacted a whale's movements. The result: the students imagined how to bring a real whale from Alaska to Tussing Elementary in Ohio. The students, with another teacher, mapped out a path along the waterways—from oceans, to rivers, to streams—which the whale might take. They considered flying the whale to the school. And they considered where the whale would stay once it got there, including the school's gymnasium and the zoo. In the end, they decided it was most appropriate to bring an artistic version of the whale to the school, and painted a mural on the walls representing the path the whale would take to get there.

The students decided the whale could stay in a large holding basin in the back of the school, which had been explored for many years by Mary's students. The project resulted in a 20-foot-high metal whale tail extending out of the grassy treeless field into the sky. A visiting artist worked with the kids and the framework Mary had established to bring the whale to life on school grounds. To further commemorate the whale's journey, a visiting musician collaborated with the kids to write a song about the whale's journey, and recorded it with the children singing along.

Mary recognizes in her students an ability to affect change, as opposed to focusing on their problems. She claims her goal is to instill in her students the ability to affect change and has implemented several service projects. She claims, "Using their numbers to talk about what we can actually do to change the world is vital."

She proudly described a fund-raising project that raised $5300 "from a community that has a lower socioeconomic level. We were thrilled with the amount of money we got, and it was turned into the Pickerington Food Pantry, which is a pantry a lot of our families use. And so it's that direct turnaround." In these and all of her lessons, Mary focuses not on what the students do not have, but what they do have and what they can do to impact the school and the world.

COLLABORATING AND ENGAGING

Collaborative art learning has tremendous opportunities for urban schools and settings. In the previous two examples, the teachers saw the potential for their students to make a difference locally. In the Florida example, high school students were encouraged to take a leadership role in examining a local need (in this case, it was often environmental), researching the issue(s) and collaboratively identifying and enacting solutions to the problem. In the Ohio example, elementary school students were engaged in long-term projects tied to big ideas and local issues that layered meaning through a depth of exploration around a particular topic. In both cases, the teachers recognized that students need to feel they belong, that they have a future, that they can leave a mark, that they have something to contribute, that they have a purpose, and that they can be a part of something bigger than themselves. Through collaboration, students can feel like part of a team. Through art-making, students can leave their mark on the world (if not their school) through personal and communal expression. And through community art learning, students can be re-engaged with school, becoming contributing members of society now and into the future.

REFERENCES

Anderson, T., & Milbrandt, M. (2005). *Art for life: Authentic instruction in art*. New York: McGraw-Hill.

Ballengee-Morris, C., & Stuhr, P. (2001). Multicultural art and visual cultural education in a changing world. *Art Education, 34*(4), 6–13.

Beckman, M. (1990). Collaborative learning: Preparation for the workplace and democracy. *College Teaching, 38*(4), 128–133.

Chickering, A. W., & Gamson, Z. F. (1991). (Eds.). *Applying the seven principles for good practice in undergraduate education*. New Directions for Teaching and Learning, No. 47. San Francisco, CA: Jossey-Bass.

Cho, M. (2006). Artistically serving: An introduction to arts-based service-learning. In R. K. Roy & M. Cho (Eds.), *My art . . . my world: A handbook on integrating service-learning into the art classroom* (pp. 1–3). Tallahassee, FL: Florida Learn and Serve.

Collier, K. G. (1980). Peer-group learning in higher education: The development of higher-order skills. *Studies in Higher Education, 5*(1), 55–62.

Cooper, J., & Associates. (1990). *Cooperative learning and college instruction*. Long Beach: Institute for Teaching and Learning, California State University.

Cooper, M., & Sjostrom, L. (2006). *Making art together: How collaborative artmaking can transform kids, classrooms, and communities*. Boston, MA: Beacon Press.

Davis, B. G. (1993). *Tools for teaching*. San Francisco, CA: Jossey-Bass.

Goodsell, A., Maher, M., Tinto, V., & Associates. (1992). (Eds.). *Collaborative learning: A sourcebook for higher education*. University Park, PA: National Center on Postsecondary Teaching, Learning, and Assessment, Pennsylvania State University.

Holloway, D. L., & Krensky, B. (2001). Introduction: The arts, urban education, and social change. *Education and Urban Society, 33*(4), 354–365.

Johnson, D. W., & Johnson, R. (1989). An educational psychology success story: Social interdependence theory and cooperative learning. *Educational Researcher, 38*(5), 365–379.

Johnson, D. W., Johnson, R. T., & Smith, K. A. (1991). *Cooperative learning: Increasing college faculty instructional productivity*. ASHE-FRIC Higher Education Report No. 4. Washington, DC: School of Education and Human Development, George Washington University.

Kohn, A. (1986). *No contest: The case against competition*. Boston, MA: Houghton Mifflin.

McKeachie, W. J., Pintrich, P. R., Lin, Y. G., & Smith, D. A. F. (1986). *Teaching and learning in the college classroom: A review of the research literature*. Ann Arbor: National Center for Research to Improve Postsecondary Teaching and Learning, University of Michigan.

Richardson, J. (2008, August). *Relatively speaking: Public collaboration and art education*. Presentation at the International Society for Education through Art conference, Osaka, Japan.

Russell, R. L., & Hutzel, K. (2007). Promoting social and emotional learning through service-learning art projects. *Art Education, 60*(3), 6–11.

Slavin, R. E. (1980). Cooperative learning. *Review of Educational Research, 50*(2), 315–342.

Slavin, R. E. (1983). When does cooperative learning increase student achievement? *Psychological Bulletin, 94*(3), 429–445.

Sleeter, C. E., & Grant, C. A. (1999). *Making choices for multicultural education: Five approaches to race, class, and gender*. Upper Saddle River, NJ: Prentice-Hall.

Whitman, N. A. (1988). *Peer teaching: To teach is to learn twice*. ASHE-ERIC Higher Education Report No. 4. Washington, DC: Association for the Study of Higher Education.

9

Artistically *Asking* About School

Picturing City Youth as Writers, Artists, and Citizens

KRISTIEN ZENKOV AND KIMBERLY SHERIDAN

Art presents the possibility of a fulfillment, which only a transformed society could offer. It is a reminder of what a truly integrated experience of oneself in society might be, a remembrance of gratification, a sense of purpose beyond alienation. Art can embody a tension which keeps hope alive . . .
—Carol Becker, "Herbert Marcuse and the Subversive Potential of Art"

Over our multiple decades working with urban youth as literacy and arts educators, we have heard innumerable students' complaints about the irrelevance of school and its assignments. While we initially dismissed these laments, we now appreciate that these grievances represent cause for concern about the tacit agreements around schooling that must exist if youth are to engage with our classes (Balfantz & Legters, 2004). In the city settings where we have worked—including Cleveland, New York, and Washington, DC—high school dropout (or "pushout") rates have registered at a minimum of 40% for the past half-century (Children's Defense Fund, 2008). These youths' persistent complaints echo their community members' multigenerational disengagement from school (Fredricks, Blumenfeld, & Paris, 2004).

But these dropout statistics do not suggest the causes of or the solutions to these embedded relationships to school. Nor do they make sense of the challenges to the social contract, which serves as the foundation of these relationships (Erickson et al., 2007). In what follows, we discuss how, using arts-based methods, we have paid attention to this contract, questions of the role of school in urban students' lives, and ways students learn to reject their educational institutions (Easton & Condon, 2009). We cannot assume students will ever know a positive relationship to school; this multigenerational rejection requires us to approach our pedagogies and the very institution of school with a critical perspective. While we exhibit faith in this social contract of schooling, in response to students' laments we now begin with the *question* of the importance of school rather than a supposition of its value (Beuschel, 2008).

THE "THROUGH STUDENTS' EYES" PROJECT

Students' literacy development plays a primary role in their decisions to remain in or drop out of school (Smyth, 2007). Recent studies have documented how schools' curricular responses to diverse populations' low traditional literacy rates contribute to school disengagement (Zenkov, 2009). Current concepts of literacy provide a responsive curricular framework through which we might engage seemingly detached youth (Christenbury, Bomer, & Smagorinsky, 2009). These insights into urban adolescents' literacies evoked the visual arts tools around which we designed the "Through Students' Eyes" (TSE) project (www.throughstudentseyes.org).

Arts-based tools are effective at enabling youth to articulate what they consider relevant to their school experiences and at promoting their writing efficacy (Marquez-Zenkov & Harmon, 2007). Visual sociologists have used image-based "photo elicitation" techniques to access adolescents' insights in ways language-centered methods cannot (Raggl & Schratz, 2004). The visual arts draw on and develop abilities to observe, envision, and explore beyond usual conceptions and capacities and reflect on that process (Hetland, Winner, Veenema, & Sheridan, 2007).

Our project has clear roots in "photovoice" and similar techniques. These methods rely on visual media to enable individuals and groups—particularly those who have been marginalized from society—to articulate their perspectives (Becker, 2001; Kress, 2006). Like "photovoice," our project is grounded in critical and feminist pedagogies, which develop youths' critical consciousness (Ewald, 2001; Harper, 2005).

With financial backing from local foundations, our high schools, and our universities, the TSE project has supplied each of approximately 100 city students with a camera with which they took pictures to answer three questions:

1. What are the purposes of school?
2. What helps you to succeed in school?
3. What gets in the way of your school success?

These youth came from our cities' most impoverished communities, composed of working-class and low-income families. While most were on track for graduation, virtually all were children of high school dropouts. The high school youth whose photographs and reflections serve as our data came from our major Midwestern city's most ethnically and linguistically diverse neighborhoods. While the project co-directors and this chapter's authors are all Caucasian, the youth participants were primarily African American, with smaller percentages of Latina/o, Asian American, and Caucasian young women and men. Our schools' dropout rates were consistently between 40% and 67%, and 9th-graders averaged below a 5th-grade reading level.

We instructed students in camera operation and modeled the "photo evaluation" process. Each youth was asked to shoot 25 to 50 images prior to each project meeting. We met biweekly across the summer in small-group and one-to-one gatherings to discuss and write about their photos. As part of the elicitation process, youth reflected on images based on their interests and the pertinence of pictures to the project's guiding questions. We transcribed young adults' oral reactions, then helped them edit their reflections on the photos they believed best answered the TSE questions.

SEEING CITY YOUTH AS CAPABLE WRITERS, ARTISTS, AND STUDENTS

The TSE project allowed young adults to engage as proficient writers and to *own* the adult-like tasks of questioning the social contract of schooling and having their responses validated as contributions to a discussion of school's purposes. Adolescents' engagement with literacy life skills has been both a product of and a mechanism of the project—outcomes and devices arts-based activities promote. The assets of our urban youths and their communities—which often go unrecognized in discussions about school and assessment—have become more apparent to us, our students, and the audiences of their work. We highlight these adult engagement and literacy themes, illustrating them with youths' images and reflections.

Alycia's Story

"Opportunity"
[The picture, "Snapshot"], makes me think of how you have one chance at life.
You can't miss your one shot. For most people if you mess up or miss your
shot, you get a second chance. In my lifestyle it's a hit or miss proposition.
That's why I go to school, education is something that I need to succeed in
my life. . . . I need to succeed in life to prove to everyone who has done me
wrong, that I am independent and just fine without them.
—Alycia Mecoli (2008)

When she took the image "Snapshot" (see Figure 9.1.), Alycia was a sophomore at a Cleveland, Ohio, high school and was involved with the summer photography and literacy "Through Students' Eyes" project. The author and her 10th-grade English teacher, Jim, had invited Alycia to participate in the project out of desperation: they never had any doubt she was a capable student, but she spent most of the year in Jim's classroom distracted by and distracting others. She was a dynamic young woman who, like so many of our students, didn't seem to know how or why she should engage in school.

Figure 9.1. "Snapshot"

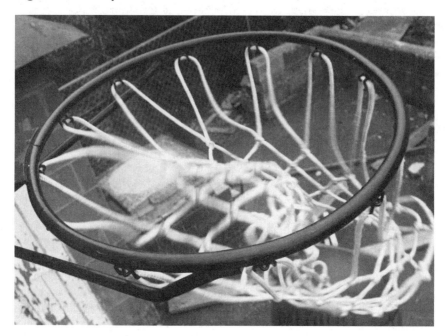

By the end of the summer, Alycia had articulated in her photography and words just why school actually did matter to her success. She shared how she had experienced considerable abuse from the men in her life and how she was estranged from a mother she still adored. She divulged how adults consistently communicated to her that they simply did not expect much of her—in school or life.

In reflections accompanying other images, she detailed her commitment to mentoring her younger siblings and neighbors—providing support from which she had never benefited. She was understandably resentful that she had not heard the affirmations she needed, but she was already offering this support to the young children close to her. This ability to serve as a mentor was an asset many of these city youth possessed. Alycia illustrated these complex ideas repeatedly, exhibiting a growing awareness that her relationships offered both positive and negative influences on her school engagement—and of how she was now ready to *choose* school's opportunities, in spite of considerable pressure to reject this institution and its priorities. Ultimately, she articulated a personal plan for school and a constructive relationship to the social contract of schooling.

Marcus's Story

"Leader"

"Leader" is a picture of my brother and he taught me everything I need to know about school and life.... [W]hen it comes down to school and my books, he constantly stays on me and teaches me to do the same for my younger brother.... He's the only person that's really been there for me.... [K]ids need role models because they need someone to set the standard on what they could be doing. My brother shows me that it's possible to put your mind to anything and accomplish it.

—Marcus Moore (2008)

Like Alycia, Marcus suggests in his image (see Figure 9.2) and text he was marginally engaged in his 10th-grade English class. Despite a very positive teacher/student rapport, his academic performance was inconsistent. We invited him to participate in the TSE project with the hope that he would discover a rationale for

Figure 9.2. "Leader"

engaging with school, find himself as a writer, and explore why school was a lower priority in his life than both he and we hoped.

Marcus was initially an erratic participant, taking pictures occasionally and showing up late for our sessions. His stance toward the project shifted, though, when a pre-service teacher, Ethan, worked with Marcus to review his images. Marcus drafted the paragraph above almost verbatim, but chose this photograph only after Ethan engaged him in conversations about his pictures. Ethan and Marcus took part in more of an interpretive critique, rather than an evaluative one (Barrett, 2003). The purpose was to gain reflective insights into what the image revealed about Marcus's ideas about how his brother was a support to him in school. These images served as a *joint* focal point for Ethan and Marcus's inquiries into how Marcus might engage with school.

Marcus clearly seemed to think we would assume his brother was incapable of serving as a positive role model because he had not finished high school. But through Ethan's facilitation, we came to appreciate the complexity of our students' role models and how these visually based processes bypassed the writing challenges these young people faced. These complex role models are an asset, which often goes unappreciated by city teachers and schools, but one Marcus readily described and illustrated. These complicated mentoring models are actually some of our youths' and their communities' strengths—borne of young people's needs and their family members' recognition that they might fill these voids.

Marcus's image and writing—from a student who had rarely composed more than a few uninspired sentences—revealed how these art-making methods elicit reflective processes, which rarely find form in school writings. This process exposed how articulate Marcus could be with the proper media and intensive guidance. Youth often find these arts-oriented processes motivating and powerful bridges to writing activities. When used in an inquiry mode, visual tools offer low barriers to traditional literacy forms, and allow young people to avoid assumptions about their negative writer identities. The TSE processes have allowed students and teachers to focus on the image first and engage in the one-to-one manner youth require if they are going to find school success. These *questions* about young adults' relationships to school call on them to invest in these relationships.

SEEING STUDENTS AS CAPABLE YOUNG ADULTS

"Realizations Of"
I took this photograph of this writing and film because this project has made me realize the importance of school. Before I kind of just blew it off and I didn't really care. . . . Now this project has really opened my eyes and my mind to how important my education really is. Ever since I started this project I feel

as if I put more effort into schoolwork and now I look forward to coming
to school every day. . . . I'm not going to get anywhere or be anybody in life
if I don't go to school. I'm proud of myself because I am doing really good in
school. Because of my grades my family is really proud of me and that's great
to know that you can make your family proud.

—Neena Massey

The reflection above (see Figure 9.3) accompanied a photograph of a blurry
page from Neena's journal from the project next to a film canister. While she was
candid about many of her thoughts and experiences, she explained that the pic-
tured journal contained personal information she did not want shared. In our
follow-up conversations with her, she described how this project had not only allowed her to reflect on the importance of school in her life, but to share her perspectives with her teachers, family members, and the audiences of our project's
publications, exhibitions, and website. Neena reminded us that schooling practices often limit teachers' opportunities to engage with struggling students in the

Figure 9.3. "Realization Of"

immediate ways they require. While these young people have very adult opinions about life and school, typical school structures and traditional teacher/student relationships limit teachers' opportunities to sufficiently honor their ideas.

These image-driven methods shifted the focus of teacher/student interactions from youths' identities as struggling students and onto their photographs. When teachers and young adults talk in sincere ways about adolescents' school-like products—their pictures—the resulting conversations are more mature than young adults typically encounter in school. These discussions focus on the *ideas* young people are considering and the *capacities* they are illustrating. Such interactions suggest the question of schooling—around which only adults typically engage—as an explicit subject for youth, in school and beyond.

Through image-based interactions, we and our students discovered a great deal about the assets to which they have access, and we learned how beginning with media enables us and youth to appreciate their ideas and writing capacities. Perhaps because they are not surrounded by peers, family members, and communities where the value of school is consistently recognized, these young people have a potentially *greater* ability to share an awareness of their relationships and the promise of this institution. Because these youth have already experienced adult-like lives, they have greater potential for appreciating school's value, and their opinions about school should be more consistently honored.

POSSIBLE IMPLICATIONS FOR SCHOOL REFORM

In our diverse city, young women and men—struggling to find purposes for engaging with school and living in communities where school's value is in question—need *studios* of adult practice if they are to become the capable writers, students, and citizens we all hope. They need to do more than experience the adult-like expectations they encounter in their intensified lives; they need classrooms that honor their perspectives and capacities and scaffold them toward success in school and beyond. Beginning with the question of school—and validating young adults' perspectives—may promote writing development, successful transitions into adulthood, and appreciation for the social contract of schooling.

Such a project is possible only when educators adopt critical perspectives on the very institution of school and recognize that its structures may not be capable of serving its young constituents. Our students' experiences in school suggest that some of the assumptions with which schools operate impede urban youths' abilities to be successful in our classrooms. This project's value extends beyond these benefits to students: young people have required us to grow as art and literacy teachers and teacher educators because their images and writing are so poignant. Our consideration of youths' responses to these questions about school motivates them to trust us and to have faith in the tacit contract of schooling. Students' photos and writings have meaning beyond our classrooms, and they suggest ideas for consequential school reforms.

Urban adolescents can offer teachers, administrators, and policymakers compelling insights about what is and what is not working in our educational institutions. Through arts-based processes we can become more aware of the literacy capacities young people possess, allowing them (and us) to move past the negative assumptions we might make about their interest in school and their abilities to find school success. One-to-one interactions with teachers motivate young people to share these perspectives. Perhaps our pedagogies should be oriented more around these intense communications. The mentoring roles youth play might serve as foundations for our teaching practices. These adolescents' adult-like responsibilities are troubling evidence they are maturing too quickly and sources for valid critiques of school engagement and achievement challenges faced by city youth. Arts-based activities oriented around challenges to the social contract of schooling allow us to interact with youth as capable students and legitimate voices in the debates about what schools and our classes should look like.

REFERENCES

Balfantz, R., & Legters, N. (2004). *Locating the dropout crisis: Which high schools produce the nation's dropouts? Where are they located? Who attends them?* Baltimore, MD: Center for Social Organization of Schools, Johns Hopkins University.

Barrett, T. (2003). *Interpreting art: Reflecting, wondering and responding.* New York: McGraw-Hill.

Becker, C. (1994). Herbert Marcuse and the subversive potential of art. In C. Becker (Ed.), *The subversive imagination: Artists, society, and social responsibility* (pp. 113–129). New York: Routledge.

Becker, H. S. (2001). Visual sociology, documentary photography, and photojournalism: It's (almost) all a matter of context. *Visual Sociology, 10*(1–2), 4–14.

Bueschel, A. C. (2008). *Listening to students about learning: Strengthening pre-collegiate education in community colleges (SPECC).* Stanford, CA: The Carnegie Foundation for the Advancement of Teaching.

Children's Defense Fund. (2008). *The state of America's children 2008.* Retrieved from www.childrensdefense.org/child-research-data-publications/data/state-of-americas-children-2008-report.html.

Christenbury, L., Bomer, R., & Smagorinsky, P. (Eds.). (2009). *Handbook of adolescent literacy research.* New York: Guilford Press.

Easton, L., & Condon, D. (2009). A school-wide model for student voice in curriculum development and teacher preparation. In A. Cook-Sather (Ed.), *Learning from the student's perspective: A secondary methods sourcebook for effective teaching.* Boulder, CO: Paradigm Press.

Erickson, F., Bagrodia, R., Cook-Sather, A., Espinoza, M., Jurow, S., Shultz, J. J., & Spencer, J. (2007). Students' experiences of school curriculum: The everyday circumstances of granting withholding assent to learn. In F. M. Connelly, M. F. He, & J. Phillion (Eds.), *Handbook of curriculum and instruction.* Thousand Oaks, CA: Sage.

Ewald, W. (2001). *I wanna take me a picture: Teaching photography and writing to children.* Boston, MA: Center for Documentary Studies/Beacon.

Fredricks, J. A., Blumenfeld, P. C., & Paris, A. H. (2004). School engagement: Potential of the concept, state of the evidence. *Review of Educational Research, 74,* 59–109.

Harper, D. (2005). What's new visually? In N. K. Denzin & Y. S. Lincoln (Eds.), *The Sage handbook of qualitative research* (3rd ed., pp. 747–762). Thousand Oaks, CA: Sage.

Hetland, L., Winner, E., Veenema, S., & Sheridan, K. (2007). *Studio thinking: The real benefits of visual arts education.* New York: Teachers College Press.

Kress, G. (2006). *Reading images: The grammar of visual design.* New York: Routledge.

Marquez-Zenkov, K., & Harmon, J. A. (2007). "Seeing" English in the city: Using photography to understand students' literacy relationships. *English Journal, 96*(6), 24–30.

Mecoli, A. (Artist). (2008). *Opportunity* [Photograph]. Cleveland, OH; "Through Students' Eyes" Project.

Moore, M. (Artist). (2008). *Leader* [Photograph]. Cleveland, OH; "Through Students' Eyes" Project.

Raggl, A., & Schratz, M. (2004). Using visuals to release pupils' voices: Emotional pathways to enhancing thinking and reflecting on learning. In C. Pole (Ed.), *Seeing is believing? Approaches to visual research* (Vol. 7, pp. 147–162). New York: Elsevier.

Smyth, J. (2007). Toward the pedagogically engaged school: Listening to student voice as a positive response to disengagement and "dropping out"? In D. Thiessen & A. Cook-Sather (Eds.), *International handbook of student experience in elementary and secondary school* (pp. 635–658). Dordrecht, The Netherlands: Springer.

Zenkov, K. (2009, Summer). The teachers and schools they deserve: *Seeing* the pedagogies, practices, and programs urban students want. *Theory Into Practice, 48*(3), 168–175.

10

Growing up Gay in the Midwest

The Youth Video OUTreach Project

MINDI RHOADES

I hear "That's so gay!" about 50 times a day. My teachers never say anything.
—Sarah

It's the first thing to say if they want to put someone down: "Oh, he's such a fag."
—Kevin

More, and younger, LGBTQ[1] students express an increased awareness of their identities, while schools are unprepared in responding (Denizet-Lewis, 2009). Many (presumed) LGBTQ youth face increased physical, emotional, and educational risks, with adult bystanders often ignoring, silencing, augmenting, and exacerbating the problems.[2] Studies continue to show LGBTQ youth with higher rates and risks for depression, suicide, substance abuse, and lower self-esteem (Denizet-Lewis, 2009; Kosciw, Diaz, & Greytak, 2010). Many LGBTQ youth are often harassed, verbally and physically; many are even assaulted. The widespread use of "That's so gay!" and "Fag!" insidiously perpetuates the daily derision, condemnation, and devaluation of LGBTQ people. In schools, while youth predominantly perpetuate this marginalization, mistreatment, and harassment, LGBTQ youth are often devastated when adults ignore, fail to respond, condone, or even participate (Blackburn, 2004; Kosciw et al., 2010). These youth often don't have the same luxury of ignoring the abuse.

Additionally, many teachers exclude LGBTQ topics, historical and biographical information, and attribution. LGBTQ students, and most others, are unlikely to receive information about the contributions of LGBTQ people across disciplinary fields, learn about LGBTQ history and struggle for civil rights, explore LGBTQ issues in assignments, and discuss current LGBTQ issues with informed LGBTQ perspectives. While it seems inconsequential, it contrasts starkly with information commonly shared with students about heterosexual scientists, artists, historical figures, issues, and perspectives. These gaps clearly affect all students, but they impact LGBTQ students in particular.

Although urban environments don't guarantee social and scholastic acceptance and support for LGBTQ youth, they often offer access to larger, more visible LGBTQ communities; a tolerant environment; and resources. These communities can provide tacit and explicit support; they can also offer assets and opportunities for LGBTQ youth to develop social, cultural, historical, and academic knowledge, skills, and networks. In stark contrast to earlier generations of LGBTQ youth, a "new kind of" LGBTQ youth is emerging who is "proud, resilient, sometimes even happy" (Savin-Williams in Denizet-Lewis, 2009). While schools may not provide LGBTQ youth with sufficient personally or culturally relevant learning opportunities, many urban environments offer creative, social, and educational opportunities for LGBTQ youth to gather, learn, and educate about LGBTQ concerns. I describe one such opportunity here.

In this chapter, I present the Youth Video OUTreach (YVO) project, with their short film *20 Straws: Growing Up Gay in the Midwest* and subsequent educational outreach program, as a successful example of applying urban arts-based critical civic praxis (Sandoval & Latorre, 2008) with LGBTQ youth. This project provides a specific example as a template for developing relevant arts-based, asset-based critical civic projects with urban youth, in or out of school, capturing the many assets available in cities.

THE YOUTH VIDEO OUTREACH PROJECT

Columbus, Ohio, currently ranks as the 16th-largest city in the United States, with over 750,000 residents. As a midsized Midwestern city, Columbus is often "underrated" in terms of its urban arts, culture, business, and educational opportunities and resources (Collins, 2010). And while Midwestern and midsized cities are often stereotyped as more homophobic than big cities, Columbus has a very large, and visible, LGBTQ population with many gay-friendly neighborhoods, businesses, community resources, and events.

Growing Up Gay "follows the lives of 9 Columbus teenagers as they come into their identities as out, gay youth. Under the guidance of video artist, Liv Gjestvang, these talented young artists share their stories of coming out and staying out in high school" (Gjestvang, 2007a, 2007b). Columbus, Ohio, video artist/activist Liv Gjestvang founded Youth Video OUTreach (YVO) in 2005 to teach LGBTQ youth digital video and production skills to create their own documentary about coming/being out in urban Midwestern high schools. Fourteen youth participants, from areas around and within the city, attended initial meetings at Kaleidoscope, a local urban LGBTQ youth center located in an urban strip mall near The Ohio State University campus. I participated in most YVO meetings, workshops, and planning sessions, serving as a teaching artist, participant, assistant, coach/mentor, and presenter.

THE SETUP: TELLING A COMPLEX STORY

We started by "looking at pretty much every video or DVD we could find about gay youth" and dissecting them as a group (Gjestvang, 2007a, 2007b). We noticed, as Gjestvang summarized, that all but one film was "an older filmmaker coming in, saying, 'I want to tell the story of gay youth.' They find some people, interview them, and then the director uses their artistic vision to create a piece." Instead, Gjestvang's goal was to enable participants "to tell their own stories in their own voices."

YVO participants wanted to acknowledge "the complicated and difficult, lonely and really hard parts" of being out, including how "homophobic language and attitudes that are pretty prevalent in high school are really hurtful and damaging." But they believed previous LGBTQ youth videos fixated too "heavily on the struggles and the really difficult side of being out," without describing the "positive story" of LGBTQ youth experiences, too (Gjestvang, 2007). They wanted to tell a fuller, more complex, more optimistic story of LGBTQ youth not completely crippled or crushed; of youth confronting, embracing, overcoming, and even erasing portions of the persistent societal stigma of being LGBTQ.

SCENE ONE: CRITICAL CONSCIOUSNESS AND GENDER GENIES

Early sessions followed a pattern alternating between learning about content and about video technology skills. We began by creating a public service announcement (PSA) about what it means to be "gay." We acknowledged being gay as an important thing about us, but not the only thing. For our PSA lines we constructed phrases: "Hi, I'm _____ and I'm (a) _____, _____, _____, and I'm _____," naming our sexual identities last.

Gjestvang started the next session with a rough compilation of these clips. Participants collectively created a complete draft of spliced statements, alternating speakers, concluding with each person's final admission. This became a template for soliciting and adding future PSA participants. Gjestvang polished an iMovie draft—adding transitions, music, and titling. After two sessions, the students completed a PSA while learning digital video basics.

Monthly weekend workshops accompanied regular meetings. A lesbian digital artist/designer specializing in local urban businesses taught digital photography basics. Using digital cameras, participants explored focus, composition, lighting, color, digital settings, and manipulation options. Gjestvang assembled their photographs from Ohio State's campus, nearby city streets, and the gay-friendly Short North Urban Arts District into a slide show for our next regular meeting.

For marginalized populations, a key component in creating relevant community change, or *critical civic praxis* (Cammarota & Ginwright, 2007), is developing critical consciousness, what Gloria Ladson-Billings calls *culturally relevant pedagogy* (1995). Pedagogies of possibility for LGBTQ youth provide safe, supportive spaces for people outside the LGBTQ community to become aware of cultural norms and their expressions, maintenance, adaptations, and enforcement (Cammarota & Ginwright, 2007). Urban environments often provide more space, resources/support, and acceptability for nontraditional behaviors and identities. Our second weekend workshop instigated a critical awareness of gender and sexual identity norms and operations.

Our particular urban LGBTQ community includes multiple groups interested in critical identity investigation—as artists, activists, performers, and academics. Two lesbian teaching artists, from our world-renowned local drag king troupe, led *The Gender Genie Workshop*, an all-day, embodied learning experience for recognizing, naming, and analyzing, and interrupting implicit/explicit gender norms.

The "Gender Genies," wearing floor-length velvety robes with seductive, sparkly metallic embroidery, cording, and matching turbans, began with us sorting words as masculine/feminine, provoking questions around language, gender, and behavior. What drives our gendered language associations? Are there benefits? Limitations? Exceptions? We discussed gender and sexual identities, heterosexism, and ways LGBTQ people disrupt traditional male/female dichotomies and hierarchies. They facilitated 30 minutes of free-writing with a gender-themed soundtrack. Then we selected bits to edit and share. While people read, we responded—nodding, cringing, sighing. We asked questions and offered comments.

Then we began an embodied exploration of gender, with Genie-supplied assortments of clothing and accessories, including a well-stocked makeup station. We explored gender costuming and performance, digitally documenting our inquiry. We modeled hats, ties, jewelry, wigs, jackets, and dresses. Two females dressed as men, with facial hair and makeup, and walked and talked "like men" to great comic effect. Another youth donned a long black wig and channeled Cher through spontaneous song.

Our workshop concluded with an impromptu field trip, filming in drag, to a nearby discount store. The youth were happy and enthusiastic, singing and skipping. Reactions included open curiosity, amusement, furtive glances, a few disapproving gazes, and some clear aversion. Security was not amused or interested in our gender-queer transgression as much as concerned with our videotaping. We were escorted, perfunctorily, out.

Redressing, we discussed ways the day's events made us more aware of culture and language perpetuating biases around gender and sexual identity norms. We contemplated suggestions about ways this knowledge might affect our work.

SCENE TWO: ALMOST ACADEMIC EXERCISES

Regular meetings focused on developing video and interview skills through personal coming-out stories. For this *academic* component, participants learned composing, editing, revising, and retaking through digital video exercises. While tasks were specific, sophisticated, and technical, participants' interest in content continued to drive their engagement; they were learning to tell *their* stories. The collaborative work and intended public nature of the film and outreach project engendered more motivation, and a much higher standard of aesthetic quality, than any grades we could have given.

To emphasize creative aspects of filmmaking, Gjestvang and her partner led a half-day weekend workshop to create visual poems. Participants created compelling representations using setting, angles, lighting, composition, and action to construct visual metaphors and impressionistic experiences. They explored locations around the city. One pair filmed a female figure running down an alley into a dead end of brown brick walls, fluttering trash remnants, and greasy black fire escapes. Another pair filmed from the passenger's seat of a car, emerging from a shadowy underpass into an explosion of city sunlight and skyscrapers. Their pieces linger in our shared experience and visual vocabulary.

Because of Columbus's size, Gjestvang and I could access multiple community connections and resources. We both work for Ohio State: me in education, Gjestvang in our Digital Union. Consequently, we could access computer hardware, software, digital equipment, human resources, and meeting space. Participants learned video skills while reviewing, arranging, and editing self-selected clips and simultaneously developing content. Facilitators individually supported participants' capturing and crafting coming-out stories into focused, coherent personal narratives. We began assembling stories into a draft for soliciting feedback on our work so far.

For our "Rough Cut" screening, Gjestvang's contacts from an urban video collective and local film festivals arranged space with a local theater on the edge of campus and near Kaleidoscope. We advertised through local LGBTQ publications, organizations, businesses, and Ohio State's College of Education courses and teacher contacts. YVO participants invited friends and family members, and sold screening tickets during our city's monthly Gallery Hop.

The "Rough Cut" screening raised funding and provided participants with feedback. The positive reception was overwhelming. Adults, many tearfully, praised participants' courage. LGBTQ adults expressed amazement at the changed environments these kids face and are creating. Other youth thanked them. Viewers asked questions—about specific scenes, stories, shots. They commented on artistic choices, offering ideas for editing and refining. One particularly confusing story line needed clarification. Some images worked well, some stories told enough, and some needed work. People also wondered what they could do, how they could help. We recorded suggestions and questions to guide our revision.

THE FINAL CUT

After 18 months, YVO completed and premiered their movie, *20 Straws*. At screenings, our most frequent question was what *20 Straws* means. During brainstorming titles, participants said being gay was "the luck of the draw," "like drawing straws," and "just who you end up being." Adults mentioned community lore that 10% of the population (1 in 10, 2 in 20) is LGBTQ. Twenty was close to their age. And drawing straws was a strong visual metaphor, inspiring the opening and closing sequences. Ta-da!

To avoid telling everyone's life stories, we created "chapters" corresponding loosely to participants' common experiences. In "Coming Out," participants describe coming out and its consequences. Denise tells her mom, who forgets; Michelle's mother tells her; and Wayne's mother responds to his handwritten confession with, "That's ok, a lot of people have that problem." Wayne balks, "Being gay is NOT a problem," but understands that that's society's constant message. "Going Out" tells the story of a lesbian couple attending prom. "Standing Out" portrays the perils of being different, including self-imposed isolation. In "Finding Out," Wayne shares excruciating childhood memories of believing he was dying because kids said all gay people had AIDS.

"Reaching Out" provides participant responses to intolerance and hatred. Andrea recounts a Pride parade where she gave a protesting child a bottle of water, telling the father, "I love you," explaining, "Whatever they may feel for me, I have no hate for them." Paul offers, "For me to want people to love and accept me for who I am, I have to love and accept them for who they are." For them, the video is a *site of healing* to reach across differences toward understanding relationships (Sandoval & Latorre, 2008, p. 90). These youth became their own advocates, reaching out, not retaliating.

Finally, "Speaking Out" recounts an incident in a nearby suburban school where a student wearing a t-shirt with stick figures holding hands and "I support gay marriage" scrawled on it was forced to remove it. More students wore similar shirts the next day; the principal insisted they change. One student refused, despite threats of escalating punishment. Over the weekend, ACLU lawyers contacted students, circulated a petition, and forced the administration to recant. The principal admitted, "Sometimes we teach the students, and sometimes they teach us" (Gjestvang & Youth Video OUTreach Collective, 2007a). For these students, LGBTQ rights activism connected them to others and to larger historical rights efforts. They agitated because they believe we're all in this together, and "It's the right thing to do."

COMMUNITY OUTREACH AND EDUCATION IMPLICATIONS

After a sold-out premiere at The Wexner Center for the Arts, *20 Straws* became the central tool for YVO's outreach component; participants shifted from learners to educators. Before completion, participants received requests for screenings and speaking engagements around Columbus. We crafted an outreach plan, including developing presentation outlines, educational materials, and resources for different age groups, organizations, and audiences; we created a scheduling system; and we began working with Columbus schools/educational institutions and local churches, organizations, and businesses. The outreach program's impact has been substantial, most notably presenting at the International Gay & Lesbian Human Rights Conference in conjunction with the World Outgames in Montreal.

Our largest impact continues to be in the urban Columbus area, primarily through Columbus City Schools and Ohio State University College of Education's urban-focused teacher education program. YVO has held screenings in local schools for gay-straight alliances (GSAs), staff meetings, classes, parent groups, school assemblies, and district-level trainings. We offered screenings and panel discussions for Ohio State's students, faculty, staff, and community. We continue to present the film as an educational tool and model for urban civic collaboration across organizations, universities, artists, and community members for addressing relevant community issues.

20 Straws has several implications for urban art education praxis. Schools can learn much from community-based organizations' (CBOs') successes by filling gaps in formal education, particularly for marginalized youth. First, support youth telling their own stories about everyday obstacles, challenges, injustices, joys, and pleasures in their lives. Second, practice culturally relevant pedagogy (Ladson-Billings, 1995) by allowing youth to learn about, and through, issues important/relevant *to them*, inspiring sophisticated, complex perspectives in critically examining *their* concerns. Third, help youth build connections and networks across similarities and differences. When traditional educational hierarchies blur, adults and youth comprise a learning community, and research and responses are collaborative. Fourth, engage community resources. More resources and educational, social, and support opportunities exist for LGBTQ youth (and other marginalized populations) in urban areas. Facilitate youth access to these. Finally, position youth as agents and educators for change. Provide them with outlets, options, and opportunities to share their creations, experiences, and knowledge, guiding them through concrete steps for positively changing their conditions. Cities provide plentiful opportunities for creating positive impact through critical civic praxis.

Like other minorities, even with more visible LGBTQ communities and resources in urban areas, gay youths' lives remain challenging and complex. Concerned community members, in conjunction with CBOs, can offer alternative venues "to acknowledge, respond to, and resolve community problems" (Ginwright, Cammarota, & Noguera, 2005, p. 25). Projects like YVO model *artivism*— urban education and activism combined through the arts—as adaptable for other organizations, populations, and schools, across subjects and age groups. Youth at any age can critically examine and confront sociocultural influences in their lives, developing and implementing plans for creating positive personal and collective change (Ballengee-Morris & Stuhr, 2001; Cammarota & Ginwright, 2007). Their educational activities can have a real, direct impact on their lives.

While *20 Straws* has not erased problems for LGBTQ youth in our city, it has been transformational. People express it at every screening—they are so thankful for the kids who made it speaking out to create change.

At the Canadian World Outgames, YVO used meeting athletes as an opportunity to augment our PSA. One athlete was Martina Navratilova. In the PSA, she ticks off her list, and at the very end, she adds, "Oh, and I almost forgot. I'm gay." That's what these kids are after—a world where you, or Martina Navratilova, could forget, or be fearless about, being gay.

NOTES

1. LGBTQ = Lesbian, Gay, Bisexual, Transgender, Queer/Questioning; used interchangeably with "gay" in this paper.
2. The Gay, Lesbian and Straight Education Network (GLSEN) 2009 National School Climate Survey, retrieved from http://www.glsen.org/.

REFERENCES

Ballengee-Morris, C., & Stuhr, P. (2001). Multicultural art and visual culture education in a changing world. *Art Education, 54*(4), 6–13.

Blackburn, M. (2004). Understanding agency beyond school-sanctioned activities. *Theory into Practice, 43*(2), 102–110.

Cammarota, J., & Ginwright, S. (2007). "Today we march, tomorrow we vote": Youth transforming despair into social justice. *Educational Foundations*, Winter-Spring, 3–8.

Collins, A. (2010). The most underrated gay-friendly cities in America. *About.com*. Retrieved from http://gaytravel.about.com/od/placestogo/tp/ underrated_gay.htm.

Denizet-Lewis, B. (September 27, 2009). Coming Out in Middle School. *The New York Times*. Retrieved from http://www.nytimes.com/2009/09/27/magazine/27out-t.html?_r=1&pagewanted=all.

Ginwright, S., Cammarota, J., & Noguera, P. (2005). Youth, social justice, and communities: Toward a theory of urban youth policy. *Social Justice*, (*32*)3, 24–40.

Gjestvang, L. (Producer) & Youth Video OUTreach Collective (Directors). (2007a). *20 Straws: Growing up Gay in the Midwest* [Motion picture]. Available from Youth Video OUTreach, 2673 Adams Avenue, Columbus, OH, 43202.

Gjestvang, L. (2007b). Press release for *20 Straws: Growing up Gay in the Midwest*. Retrieved from http://web.me.com/liv.gjestvang/YouthVideoOUTreach/ About.html.

Kosciw, J. G., Diaz, E. M., & Greytak, E. A. (2010). *The 2009 National School Climate Survey: The experiences of lesbian, gay, bisexual, and trans-gender youth in our nation's schools*. New York: Gay, Lesbian and Straight Education Network.

Ladson-Billings, G. J. (1995). Toward a theory of culturally relevant pedagogy. *American Education Research Journal, 35*, 465–491.

Sandoval, C., & Latorre, G. (2008). Chicana/o artivism: Judy Baca's digital work with youth of color. In A. Everett (Ed.), *Learning Race and Ethnicity: Youth and Digital Media* (pp. 81–108). The John D. and Catherine T. MacArthur Foundation Series on Digital Media and Learning. Cambridge, MA: The MIT Press.

11

Empowering Youth Culture

Possibilities for Creating a Teen Museum

CAROL NG-HE

> Teen culture is the lifestyle, environment, or traditions a teen may experience.
> Teens face many issues such as identity, family problems, and finding the right
> crowd. Their environment is chaotic and wild; much like animals. Now how do
> young artists like us showcase this?
> —The Chicago Teen Museum, *Teen Made Museum*

The Chicago Teen Museum is the first museum of its kind dedicated to the preservation of teen culture. In this chapter I will investigate teen culture in historical and artistic contexts and map out existing initiatives, which explore teen culture by connecting teens to museums and art-making in museums. By reviewing teen participants at the Chicago Teen Museum, I suggest museum-making as a new art practice and propose integrating museum-making into urban schools.

WHAT IS "TEEN CULTURE"?

To define "teen culture," a teen participant from the Chicago Teen Museum's previous program wrote: "Teen culture is the lifestyle, environment, or traditions a teen may experience" (The Chicago Teen Museum, 2009). According to Jon Savage (2007), in his book *Teenage: The Creation of Youth Culture*, the beginning of teen culture can be traced back to the 19th century Industrial Revolution, with changes in social and familial structures. Labor demand in cities brought teens into the world of work, away from consistent parental supervision. Savage credited American social psychologist Stanley Hall for coining the term "adolescence" in the late 19th century, emphasizing a view of teen stresses and strains justifying the need for special care and attention. As Europe entered the era of World War II in the 20th century, Savage described German teens turning to the Nazi regime in search of patriotism and inquiry, and for a sense of purpose and status. In the next decade, during the post–World War II period, American youth triumphantly defined teen culture with the consumption of modern materialism. From the mid-20th century on, as a teen from our program precisely pointed out, "teens face many issues such as identity, family problems, and finding the right crowd. Their environment is chaotic and wild; much like animals" (The Chicago Teen Museum, 2009, p. 17).

While examination of the historical development of teen culture is available, there is very limited documentation centralizing collections of art created by teenagers and recognition of their artistic merits across time, geographic locations, and cultures. One exception is the Alliance for Young Artists & Writers, a nonprofit organization that "identifies teenagers with exceptional artistic and literary talent and brings their remarkable work to a national audience through The Scholastic Art & Writing Awards" (The Alliance for Young Artists & Writers, n.d.).

MAPPING INVOLVEMENT OF TEENS IN MUSEUMS

In Chicago, there are a number of major venues producing or presenting teens' work as professional productions. One example is Yollocalli Arts Reach, located in the heart of Pilsen, near the south side of Chicago, with a high population of Mexican Americans. Yollocalli Arts Reach is a youth initiative of the National Museum of Mexican Art, highlighting arts education and career training for teens and young adults. Yollocalli has partnered with various local organizations, including After School Matters, the Chicago Park District, and local schools to create "an open forum for experimentation in art-making based on issues in art, history, and youth culture" (Yollocalli Arts Reach, n.d.). Among their many projects, *Youth Curators/Youth Gallery* shared the Chicago Teen Museum's vision of giving teens the opportunity to act as museum professionals and curators to collaboratively create an exhibition reflecting their community. The Chicago History Museum's Teen Chicago Council, conducted from 2003 to 2004, aimed to incorporate teens' perspectives in the search for oral histories from individuals about growing up in Chicago during the 20th century (The Chicago History Museum's Teen Council, n.d.). The Museum of Contemporary Art Education Department and the Art Institute of Chicago Teen Lab reached out to city teens to include their artwork in the Museum of Contemporary Art's *All-City Art Exhibit*. The exhibit presented teen artwork by students attending the Chicago Public Schools (CPS), was curated by the MCA Curatorial Coordinator, and was on view at the museum and the Illinois Institute of Technology. In 2006, at the Teen Lab of the Art Institute of Chicago in collaboration with After School Matters, 14 Teen Lab members worked together to create the first-ever teen-produced museum guide, in which they selected artworks from the museum's collection and reinterpreted the artworks through written and visual forms.

On a national level, cultural institutions are becoming increasingly aware of the necessity of teen voice in organizational development. As such, they are establishing teen councils where teens take on advisory roles to museums and gain hands-on experience in conceiving, designing, and producing artwork in museums. Some notable places include the Walker Art Center Teen Arts Council (Minneapolis, Minnesota), the Bronx Museum of the Arts Teen Council (New York, New York), the Museum of Modern Art (MoMA) Red Studio (New York, New York), and the Alliance for Young Artists and Writers Galleries (New York, New York). Calder Zwicky, who is currently a community outreach consultant to museums, made the following remarks on the blog of MoMA P.S.1. (formerly P.S.1. Contemporary Art Center) about his participation as a Teen Arts Council member for the Walker Art Center in his youth:

> That fall, when I was sixteen, the Walker started the Teen Arts Council. As one of the initial group of students, I remember the feeling of being involved in something that was creating its own rules and goals as we went along . . . Filled with confidence and real-world experience, I went on to attend college, did well, graduated, and began working as a visual artist . . . In 2005 I became the educator in charge of running the Bronx Museum of the Arts' first-ever Teen Council, a position I maintain to this day . . . My current life, therefore, feels very connected to my time on the Teen Arts Council. Rarely a day goes by that I don't explicitly reference something I learned from my own involvement in teen programs . . . When you're a teenager, who you are is still in flux, and as a result the future can seem terrifying. Coming to terms with your identity as an artist and your place within the art world is daunting, even for adults . . . it falls on us as cultural institutions to . . . create safe, creative environments for this next generation of artists to flourish. Their work looks good, man. We should put it up in our Museum. (Zwicky, 2010).

Calder exemplified the reciprocal impacts of teen involvement to both teens and the museums in strengthening their educational role. To support the potential of teens and museums, I offer a pedagogy of teen involvement deployed by the Chicago Teen Museum. I further explore collaborative potentials of a teen-driven museum in the context of urban schools.

WHY THE CHICAGO TEEN MUSEUM?

The Chicago Teen Museum's director, Erin Dragotto, recognizes the growing population of teens, suggesting that there are 34 million people between the ages of 12 and 19 in the United States. She sees now as a critical time to start a museum for and by teens to offer a place and opportunity where they are active contributors to society. "What better way to creatively showcase teen opinion, preserved through exhibits and programs, and on view for the public, than in a cultural institution

teens can call their own?" (personal interview, 2010). Currently, the 4-year-old organization is staffed by three members, including a director, a program developer
and teaching artist, and a grant writer, with the support of the board and a number
of adult volunteers, as well as Teen Council members who provide ongoing advice
in program planning. As an emerging teen-based museum, the organization currently exists virtually and through partnerships for physical space. It is our long-
term goal to have a physical space rooted in the community of Chicago.

The Making

The Chicago Teen Museum (CTM) introduces teens to museum-making as a
means of artistic practice. Our pedagogy is grounded on the following principles:

1. *Teen empowerment.* Our programs aim to bring different life experiences
   of teens from their families, schools, and communities, for inspiration
   and reference in the art projects at the CTM. In addition, we embrace the
   idea of "teens in charge," in recognizing teens' ability to re-envision an
   institution celebrating their culture. We see our programs as a form
   of arts activism education; we ask teens to envision how schools/
   neighborhoods/communities/organizations shape them.
2. *Museum-making.* Our organizational philosophy and programming
   are based on the practice of "crossing": crossing generations, crossing
   neighborhoods, crossing time, and crossing aspirations or professions. A
   teen from a previous summer program suggested the necessity of a teen
   museum:

   > This museum will show others that teens are just the same as famous artists out
   > there, maybe even better than them. This museum can offer a lot to its viewers
   > like it can open your mind, make you explore more things, *become a different
   > person* . . . I hope it will also let others see that not all teens are alike in any way.
   > We each have something new to bring to the table and that table is the Chicago
   > Teen Museum. (Personal interview, 2009, italics added for emphasis)

3. *Connection-making.* In addition to teens, the programs also involve museum
   professionals, nonprofit leaders, parents, and school administrators. Our
   Teen Council gathers teens from across the city who may not be able to
   meet otherwise. Having teens take part in the council offers them the
   opportunity to foster positive relationships with their peers and develop
   a new community.

Teen Council members serve an advisory role in conceptualizing exhibit themes.
An active member of our Teen Council, Jessica Schapiro, 17, recalled her experience serving on the Council:

In determining the conceptual focus of the museum, we filled sheet after sheet of butcher paper up with things that we wanted to explore. A lot of the ideas are very personal, not things that you're going to find in a textbook or a newspaper. And we found that we wanted to explore them through personal stories, narratives, and anecdotes, rather than facts and anecdotes like you would find in a science museum. (What Kids Can Do, 2009)

In mobilizing teens to rethink the values of their work as contributing to contemporary teen culture, we have developed two main approaches to developing a teen museum. The first approach is through partnerships with schools and their physical spaces, and the second approach is using the Internet as a virtual space.

School Space

The Chicago Teen Museum has partnered with After School Matters and the Chicago Academy for the Arts, an independent arts-based high school, to implement our first summer art education program. Based on self-inquiry and exploration, the project highlights themes relating to self, community, and society. Nearly 30 teens were introduced to making a museum model using cardboard, charcoal drawing, and acrylic painting to depict personal aspirations and challenges. They also created small-scale installation art using a shoebox and created a personal artist/curatorial statement to reflect their ideal teen museum space.

First, we explored space, a key in creating a teen made museum. The teens explored how some contemporary artists innovated a space to speak of their own fantasy of utopia. We visited the Museum of Contemporary Art in downtown Chicago to explore the exhibit on Buckminster Fuller's utopian architecture and Olafur Eliasson's temporal installation art. After the trip, the teens discussed what space meant for the artists and ways the space engaged the audience. In response, the teens developed a symbol reflecting a hobby, interest, or aspiration. They then collaboratively developed a three-dimensional model of their ideal museum space to exemplify contemporary teen culture. At the end of the summer program, the teens curated their own show, "Teens' Space," at the high school.

The teens developed subtitles and wrote descriptions of their artworks on display. Their curatorial statement summarizes the exhibit:

"Teens' Space" was created by teens to give a voice. Museums today do not give good representation of teenagers. We created this exhibit to represent ourselves and let other individuals know about this particular age group. Through creativity and teamwork, we created an exhibit to present ourselves to the public. In the process, we visited other museums and drew inspiration from past artists to guide us in the layout and the design of the museum. As teens it is very important for us to have our own museum, because the transition from child to adult known as teenage years is essential to every person's life. Our artwork expresses the lifestyle that teens face. (The Chicago Teen Museum, 2009, p. 43)

The outcome of this 8-week summer program affirmed possibilities of a museum for, by, and about teens. The responses we have received also continue to motivate us to further engage with teens in creating their own museum spaces. They are not only the artists, culture producers, exhibit curators, and visionaries who build the conceptual foundation for the Chicago Teen Museum; they are the museum-makers.

Virtual Space

While public presence of teen artwork is limited, there is increasing interest and popularity of teen-made online publications. As American teens are immersed in cyberculture, the virtual space represents a powerful and effective communication engine for mobilizing teens. The Chicago Teen Museum's website (www .chicagoteenmuseum.org) is intended to serve as a virtual studio—a studio for teens to discuss, produce, and display their creative works. As Erin Dragotto suggests, our website provides resources and advice to museum constituents, educators, school administrators, and principals about teen trends, and centralizes academic research and resources on teen culture. In addition, museum professionals and cultural workers can use this virtual studio for collaboration on curriculum writing and project development (Dragotto, 2010).

THE TEEN MUSEUM AND CITY SCHOOLS

The city was integral to the formation and development of the Chicago Teen Museum. Cities provide critical resources from which a teen museum could be developed elsewhere. For example, violence in the Chicago area was a major issue our teens wanted to explore, as well as how it has leaked into the public school system. This led to a deeper examination and critique on teens' views about parenting, current school structure, teacher training, peer pressure, and stress on teenagers. Most importantly, the city provided a platform for teens to consider *how* these combined factors affect teens, and resources available in their city. With this in mind, the Chicago Teen Museum works to develop collaborative opportunities with other local museums, urban high schools, and cultural institutions to materialize CTM teens' interest in researching social issues and city resources.

It is not enough to merely talk about the importance of school–museum collaboration for teen audiences; museums in the 21st century need to rethink and reposition teens toward active leadership. After all, adolescence is a defining life stage deserving of special care and attention. Engaging teens to be museum leaders affirms their social status and values their creative outputs. It also provides positive community support and revolutionizes the way museums are developed and the way urban high schools can engage students.

REFERENCES

The Alliance for Young Artists and Writers. (n.d.). Retrieved from http://www.artandwriting.org.

The Chicago History Museum's Teen Council. (n.d.). Retrieved from http://www.chicagohistory.org/static_media/pdf/teenChicago/CHM-TeenChicagoCurriculum Guide.pdf

The Chicago Teen Museum. (2009). *Teen made museum*. Chicago: Author.

Dragotto, E. Personal communication, May 30, 2010.

Frank, A. (1993). *Anne Frank: The diary of a young girl*. New York: Bantam.

Savage, J. (2007). *Teenage: The creation of youth culture*. New York: Viking Adult.

What Kids Can Do. (2009). *A teen made museum: Chicago youth interpret teen cultures*. Retrieved from http://www.whatkidscando.org/your_stories/2010/04_teen_made_museum/index.html.

Yollicalli Arts Reach. (n.d.). *Youth curators/Youth gallery*. Retrieved from http://youthcurators.blogspot.com.

Zwicky, C. (March 15, 2010). My life in museums: The importance of community outreach and teen programs. *MoMa, PS1 Blog*. Retrieved from http://www.moma.org/explore/inside_out/2010/03/15/my-life-in-museums-the-importance-of-community-outreach-and-teen-programs/#more-4433.

12

Sacred Structures

A Constructivist Elementary School Art Studio Project

JAMES HAYWOOD ROLLING JR.

> The question comes up whether to teach the structure, or to present the
> child with situations where he is active and creates the structure himself. The
> goal in education is not to increase the amount of knowledge, but to create
> the possibilities for a child to invent and discover. When we teach too fast, we
> keep the child from himself inventing and discovering. Teaching means creating
> situations where structures can be discovered; it does not mean transmitting
> structures which may be assimilated at nothing other than a verbal level.
> —Jean Piaget, unpublished remarks, quoted by Eleanor Duckworth,
> in Hawkins, 2002

Oliver, one of my 2nd-grade students during the spring of 2004, related the meaning he had meticulously embedded into his replica of a cathedral, during a videotaped interview with me. Oliver worked before class, between classes, and after classes on completing his model in time for the opening of our Museum of Sacred Spaces, a temporary exhibition of structures designed and assembled by each of my 2nd-grade students during our yearlong study of the theme "Me and My Community." But it was during my interview of Oliver that he related meanings incorporated into his structure that were not apparent to me during the learning and construction process. Having removed the roof from his handmade miniature cathedral, Oliver was explaining—from a bird's-eye point of view—the significance of the intersection of the row of pews along the nave as it cut between the two mirroring transepts in his cross-shaped floor plan, and intersected the blue and white wave-like floor patterns he had carefully inlaid within the transepts with interlocking colored beads.

Oliver (explaining the floor patterns): It's kind of like a symbol for the
 ocean.
Me: . . . Okay. Oh, is that why it has those waves?

Oliver: Yeah, kind of wavy . . . And then . . . there's also a story . . . about
the water's separation . . .

Me (surprised): Oh . . .

Oliver: And, so this would be the . . . Egypt, or something . . . (pointing
forward at the very rear of the nave at the main entry into the cathedral
and then dragging his finger back toward himself, tapping along
the neatly aligned row of wooden pews he had cut using the mitre
box) . . . and then water would be flowing here . . . (swirls his hands
within both transepts, bringing them together above the center of the
main aisle.)

Me: Right . . .

Oliver: But, it's a cross, so you can always go to wherever you want.

Me: So that's a symbol of the parting of the ocean so that, um, the people of
God could get through.

Oliver: Yeah.

Me: Wow, that's a deep . . . that's a really . . . I didn't even know that you
did that.

Oliver: (Chuckles)

Me: That's one of those hidden meanings that I didn't even know that was
there.

RETHINKING WHAT KIDS DO IN ART CLASS

Making meaning is a learned behavior (Narey, 2009). We learn to construct meaning early in our childhood and continue to do so the rest of our lives. We construct
our identities as well as our societies. Many art teachers spend a great deal of time
either giving students assignments that will occupy them, or trying to get them
to behave positively—as if "doing" and "productive behavior" were not entirely
linked. The key to activating this linkage is to engage learners in doing things that
they feel positive about in ways open to divergent and individually determined
learning outcomes. According to Marsha Grace (1999), "(s)ocial-constructivist
teaching and learning is nonconformist, open to variation in the outcome of what
has been learned" (p. 50).

Consequently, making meaning in the art classroom is inherently an asset-
based activity wherein a learner's development cannot be predetermined, a facet
of the basic human effort to generate and sustain personal and social growth. The
arts' practices, in particular, are meaning-making behaviors that typically manifest
themselves in one or a combination of three distinct ways: "making marks," "making models," or "making special."

A meaningful concept is analogous to a piece of architecture—the process
of meaning-making amalgamates some elements of present experience and prior

knowledge into a recognizable and recallable edifice, representing a particular understanding at a given time. To make meaning is like conceiving the right word to fit a sentence. However, meaning-making is part of the dynamic activity of general *sense-making*, which allows for the continual reassembly of prior meanings—rearrangements of the current architecture of meaning, current usages, and current developmental possibilities. My definition of the term "sense" is extrapolated from Lev Semenovich Vygotsky's discussion of the difference between the "meaning" of a word and the "sense" of a word:

> Meaning is only one of the zones of the sense that a word acquires in the context of speaking . . . The real [application of the] meaning of a word is not constant. In one operation a word emerges in one meaning and in another it takes on another meaning. This dynamism of meaning leads us to . . . the problem of the relationship of meaning and sense. The word considered in isolation and in the lexicon has only one meaning. But this meaning is nothing more than a potential that is realized in living speech. In living speech this meaning is only a stone in the edifice of sense. (Vygotsky, cited in Wertsch, 1985, p. 124)

New word components—or new elements of meaning—can be substituted in, revised, or translated across language barriers; nevertheless, the general sense will remain discernable. This is analogous to the sense we make of our urban landscapes. Whenever a new physical edifice or component of meaning is constructed, we are compelled to make sense of our changing contexts and their relationship to one another all over again. Whether we speak of the city we live in or learning in the art studio, every piece of architecture and every remaining void is thus an asset toward the continuing development of the general communal value we must make and remake.

The purpose of this chapter is to rethink arts education practice in a way that will challenge educators and stakeholders in public education to change the way we see art-making in schools, the way we see the urban landscape, and the way we see curriculum in the urban and inclusive classroom.

THE SOCIAL SIGNIFICANCE OF MAKING MARKS, MAKING MODELS, AND MAKING SPECIAL

Arts practices are self-organizing behaviors through which humans construct systems of meaning utilizing medium-specific, language-specific, and/or critical methodologies, all with informational consequences (Rolling, 2008). The arts organize and *inform* our collective sense of ourselves, our contexts, and our place in the world. Whether we are referring to the rudimentary and random crayon scribbles in childhood or the initial scrawled letters of early literacy development (Danko-McGhee & Slutsky, 2007; Narey, 2009), the first among these behaviors to be manifested can be termed as "making marks."

"Making marks" indicates presence, carving out a niche within current circumstances and context that says, "I am here." To make marks is to initiate local change, an exertion of a young learner's emergent control over sense-making tools within their environment.

Subsequent to early mark-making behavior, there emerges in the learner the ability to make models of their sensory experiences, perceptions, and ideas. Whether collecting seemingly incongruous rocks, artifacts, and species from the backyard into a shoebox or drawing a still life, "making models" indicates comprehension, constituting an order out of current circumstances and context that says, "I shape microcosms."

Ellen Dissanayake (2003) introduces the idea of the arts as the evolutionary practice of "making special" that which is claimed as significant to the ongoing life of individuals, societies, and civilizations. Dissanayake redefines the larger purpose of making art as the development of a network of systems for organizing and perpetuating behaviors through which humans make "special" the ideas, actions, events, and/or materials for which they have a natural need or selected affinity. When selected ideas, practices, or objects are identified as having life-sustaining value, making art of such things makes it possible to render them as totems, stimulating an empathetic social response that draws other humans to self-organize around them as well. "Making special" indicates agency, re-presenting current circumstances and contexts in a way that delineates identity, home, and community and says, "I make a difference here."

THE ASSETS INHERENT IN STUDENTS' MAKING-MEANING

Too often, what goes on in the art classroom is viewed in a delimiting fashion, as kids either making "children's art" or merely mimicking the work of adults. Actually, learners are exceeding our expectations; they are making meaning. Each opportunity to make meaning is like a hook and ladder in constructing the latticework of the learner's cognitive development (Efland, 1995, 2002). Students simply need teachers willing to collaborate with them and help them make sense of what they have accomplished.

I was hired to teach and design curriculum in early 2003 as part of the faculty of a brand-new elementary school in New York City, right after the completion of my doctoral studies in education. In our 1st academic year, those of us on the 2nd-grade teaching team linked trimester studies on "Structure," "Custom," and "Expression" together in succession within our ambitious yearlong thematic exploration. The unit of study described in this chapter began with a focus on the structure of our school, on architecture in our neighborhood, and ultimately on local cultural celebrations and rituals, with field trips to religious buildings and spaces that hosted them.

In April 2004, as we were transitioning from "Custom" to "Expression" trimester studies, I began this arts learning unit by asking our 2nd-grade students to reflect on and describe activities within their own life experiences that they wished to depict as "sacred." For the sake of simplicity, the term "sacred" was presented as an activity, belief, or object one considers so special that one might build a structure devoted to practicing, recognizing, or preserving it. Our aim was to spend the next several weeks building carefully realized models of these structures.

Earlier in the year during a unit on the building and structure of our school, I had worked with one classroom of 2nd-graders to measure out and construct an accurate scale model of the floor in our new building that housed the 2nd-grade classrooms, so students were already familiar with some of the challenges of model construction (see Figure 12.1). Prior to my degrees in the visual arts and education, I studied architecture and had even practiced as a freelance architectural model-maker. Therefore, I was ultimately building on my own assets and experience to facilitate this unit. We primarily used wood, cardboard, and foamcore—common model-making materials.

Figure 12.1. Second-grade students at The School erecting one wall in a scale model.

I presented students with some slide shows on our Smart Board (an interactive, electronic whiteboard) depicting how specific shapes, colors, numbers, and pieces of architecture (i.e., bridges, doorways or gates, windows, etc.) could all be used as symbols representing other special things. After some initial dialogue on symbolic meaning, students filled out simple worksheets I created for them to describe a use for a sacred structure they might build for special purposes all their own. I emphasized throughout that any symbolic architectural features, shapes, colors, and/or numbers they selected could either be hidden or made obvious in the structure to make it more meaningful. In order to be able to later reflect upon all this meaning-making activity, the worksheets I provided allowed students to record their symbol choices. At this point, students were given the go-ahead to begin construction.

Oliver, more than any other student in my 2nd-grade classes sought to collaborate with me on how to bring the removable three-dimensional high-peaked roof he had envisioned (complete with a rose window above the main door) into reality. Oliver did all of his own measurements on the cross-shaped floor plan, windows, roof, and walls of his structure. Given his age, I handled any cutting or incisions involving a matte knife, and Oliver handled any cutting and prefabrication that involved a pair of scissors or the small portable paper cutter, with my supervision.

Each sacred structure represented a divergent outcome, no two looking alike or holding the same meanings. Each was temporarily displayed in our own in-school Museum of Sacred Spaces. As I surveyed the collection, it became apparent to me that I needed to document the students' reflections on the story of each structure. I compiled a videotaped log of the 2nd-graders explaining the significance of their structures in what I called "The Sacred Structures Interviews" and posted it on the school's network server for general access. In the interviews, I asked the students to reflect on the symbols embedded in their sacred constructs. Fascinatingly, these one-on-one dialogues often served to proliferate new episodes of meaning-making as the students recounted the details of their work. Several of the students were also engaging in storytelling—discovering and elaborating on emergent significance as they *revisited* and *reinterpreted* intended meaning.

Arthur sculpted a pointed dome-like structure that protrudes above a primeval lake with a single access bridge leading to its doorway. Its pyramidal shape was intended to symbolize "strength" and the newfound ability he was cultivating and quite proud of, the capacity to "carry on" from the brink of anger and return himself to a place of peace. Nabila's sacred structure was a suite of rooms for meditation or yoga beneath a translucent roof of blue tissue paper raised high upon columns, an exuberant tour de force that recalled our field trip to the Islamic Cultural Center on Manhattan's Upper East Side. Nabila even included built-in shelves to place one's shoes and "keep the carpet clean" as one prepares for prayer. Arielle created "a ritual room" paying homage to a ritual involving paper butterflies she held prominently in her memory. Each sacred structure offered evidence that learning "is the process of making sense or creating meaning from experience" (Narey, 2009, p. 2).

The varying life experiences and perceptions of my students quite naturally led to divergent project outcomes. But when we also consider that the dense interaction of urban living is itself generative of divergent and uncommon experiences, dwelling in inner-city urban contexts can be properly viewed as a ready asset to public education and curriculum reform, rather than a disadvantage each learner must overcome.

MAKING NEW SENSE OF THE SACRED IN THE CITY

In order to change the way we see the urban landscape in the context of urban education, it is advantageous to see the urban environment as more than just an extension of the classroom. It is also as a precursor to classroom learning experiences and a potential repository for the outcomes of classroom learning. A city may in itself be considered a repository of the evidence of social learning, or the lack thereof. For instance, in any given city, you might view the visual exemplars of unlearned lessons regarding race, social justice, and community calcified into rigid neighborhood divisions marginalizing large, impoverished segments of the populace. Or you might see evidence of a city that is a work in progress, with areas previously blighted now in the midst of a revitalization of economic strength and public traffic.

A city serves as a primary site for rapidly constructing and re-signifying relationships "between people and other living and non-living forms" (Blandy & Hoffman, 1993, p. 24). Embracing this idea can lead to learning opportunities like those on display in Project Row Houses, a 20-year-old urban public arts effort envisioned and launched by artist and community activist Rick Lowe when he and a coalition of other artists bought and repurposed a row of 22 derelict shotgun houses originally built in the 1930s (Kimmelman, 2006).

Project Row Houses is located in the Third Ward, a predominantly low-income African American neighborhood in Houston, Texas. Lowe treated this phalanx of row houses as "found objects" that stood as emblems of the urgency and significance of "home" in the Third Ward. As I interpret it, Lowe and his coalition of artists marked the row houses in a sense as *sacred*—as a space signified and set apart from other places in its transcendence of everyday experience and expectations.

Through this effort, a neglected facet of the Third Ward was reinterpreted as the home to a community-based international artist residency program and studio/gallery spaces; a young mothers residential program; new duplex housing units; and a new local nightspot and other revenue-producing urban renewal ventures. Lowe is quoted as adamant in having no intention of reproducing Project

Row Houses elsewhere, revealing his clear understanding that what is sacred in one locality may not be life-sustaining or symbolic of the local life anywhere else (Kimmelman, 2006). Nevertheless, the great potential here is not in replicating this particular project, but rather in its approach to the city as a place where what has been learned is openly reinterpreted. It is this synthetic process that can be replicated in any classroom.

Ultimately, the search for the sacred in the city is an asset-based approach to education in our urban contexts, one that does not view city living as a bevy of dangers to be survived, but as an environment our students are already successfully making sense of how to live in (Asher, 2000).

URBAN ASSETS, URBAN POSSIBILITIES

In order to change the way we view curriculum-making in the urban classroom, it becomes important to generate a continuum of new possibilities, leveraging the assets learners bring to the classroom as they negotiate multiple edifices of sense in the engagement of meaning-making. I am interested in urban living and in how we may learn to signify our own personal shelters—placeholders for our distinct identities—out of a sprawling urban complexity that never ceases to take shape. The construction and reinterpretation of an edifice of sense, or "home," for personal identity is crucial in the construction of the concept of "community," since community is the extension of "home" into the local commons—an area of shared needs, problems, and opportunities. By inviting learners to narratively reflect on the places and ideas they have personally signified as integral to their identity (i.e., as "sacred"), an "art education of place" (Blandy & Hoffman, 1993, p. 23) is also reconceptualized as a process, not just a position.

The purpose and shape of urban environments are reconstituted from continual placements, displacements, and replacements of building footprints and edifices. With each iteration, what matters most is reconsidered. Urban arts education pedagogy should likewise be practiced as a meaning-making endeavor, trumping prior expectations of a classroom of learners to reveal what matters most to each across varying edifices of sense and multiple systems for constructing sense (Kindler, 1999). A reconceptualized urban arts education practice yields possibilities for a continuum of learning that may be initiated in schools, at home, throughout the city, and beyond.

REFERENCES

Asher, R. (2000). The Bronx as art: Exploring the urban environment. *Art Education, 53*(4), 33–38.

Blandy, D., & Hoffman, E. (1993). Toward an art education of place. *Studies in Art Education, 35*(1), 22–33.

Danko-McGhee, K., & Slutsky, R. (2007). *The impact of early art experiences on literacy development.* Reston, VA: National Art Education Association.

Dissanayake, E. (2003). *Homo aestheticus: Where art comes from and why.* Seattle, WA: University of Washington Press.

Efland, A. D. (1995). The spiral and the lattice: Changes in cognitive learning theory with implications for art education. *Studies in Art Education, 36*(3), 134–153.

Efland, A. D. (2002). *Art and cognition: Integrating the visual arts in the curriculum.* New York: Teachers College Press.

Grace, M. (1999). When students create curriculum. *Educational Leadership, 57*(3), 49–52.

Hawkins, D. (2002). *The informed vision: Essays on learning and human nature.* New York: Algora Publishing.

Kimmelman, M. (2006, December 17). In Houston, art is where the home is. *The New York Times.* Retrieved from http://www.nytimes.com/2006/12/17/arts/design/17kimm.html.

Kindler, A. M. (1999). "From endpoints to repertoires": A challenge to art education. *Studies in Art Education, 40*(4), 330–349.

Narey, M. (Ed.). (2009). *Making meaning: Constructing multimodal perspectives of language, literacy, and learning through arts-based early childhood education.* New York: Springer.

Rolling, J. H. (2008). Rethinking relevance in art education: Paradigm shifts and policy problematics in the wake of the information age. *International Journal of Education & the Arts, 9* (Interlude 1). Retrieved from http://www.ijea.org/v9i1/.

Wertsch, J. V. (1985). *Vygotsky and the social formation of mind.* Cambridge, MA: Harvard University Press.

13

Beyond Interpretation

Responding Critically to Public Art

MELANIE L. BUFFINGTON AND ERIN WALDNER

> Every day I traverse a busy urban street in Richmond, Virginia home to
> numerous public sculptures. Along my way, I frequently see Richmond Public
> School busses driving to various destinations. I also pass several museums and
> see large school groups heading toward the science, history, children's, or art
> museum. Yet, I have never seen a school group using the large public sculptures,
> an obvious part of the urban environment, as a formal part of their learning.
> Why are formal institutions a popular educational resource, but not public art?
> —Melanie Buffington, personal notes, 2010

Access to public art in cities is an asset for students in urban schools. Argiro (2004) and Russell (2004) both urge art educators to take advantage of public art as original artwork for students to experience in person. Public art provides an opportunity to study local history and practice interpretation. Further, critical research into local public art can provide urban students with an opportunity to agree or disagree with the ways public art in their community portrays local identity. We propose a curriculum framework, the *critical response cycle*, based on a study of local public art that goes beyond interpretation by engaging students in understanding, reclaiming, and adding new meanings to existing public sculpture. By using public art as a central focus for studying a city, students can develop tools to reclaim and rewrite meanings embedded in public artworks they regularly encounter.

The *critical response cycle* utilizes aspects of participatory action research, asset-based community development, and urban critical pedagogy and functions as a flexible framework to study public art in various cities.

Participatory action research (PAR) is a methodology frequently utilized by educators working from a critical theory perspective involved in purposive change-oriented work (Haney & Lykes, 2010). In a PAR study, the researcher is an active member of the group, not an objective observer. Rather than conducting research *on subjects*, a researcher conducts the study *with participants*. In this way, the authoritative outsider role of the researcher is exchanged for a mode of research that recognizes multiple perspectives and values participants' voices.

Asset-based community development (ABCD) is a strategy of neighborhood revitalization that utilizes a community's existing assets rather than supplying outside services to remedy perceived needs (Kretzmann & McKnight, 1993). Kretzmann and McKnight urge that all assets be considered, including individual talents of community members, community associations, local institutions, and physical resources of the geographical location. In ABCD, community members are the primary actors in all phases of development projects and work toward building their own community, not perceiving themselves as recipients of outside assistance.

Much talk about urban education focuses on deficiencies and challenges. This negative focus may be one factor holding urban schools back. Because urban schools and students are all unique, imposing a fixed curriculum from the outside may not be successful (Duncan-Andrade & Morrell, 2008). How could art teachers use PAR and ABCD to build meaningful curriculum with urban students?

In the following chapter, we explore the framework's foundations and outline the critical response cycle steps. Finally, we offer suggestions for how to implement this pedagogy by considering two markedly different works of public art in two different cities.

FRAMEWORK FOR RECLAIMING AND CRITICALLY RESPONDING TO PUBLIC ART

Influenced by scholarly work from fields including art education (Argiro, 2004; Russell, 2004), sociology (Loewen, 1999), community development (Kretzmann & McKnight, 1993), and education (Duncan-Andrade & Morrell, 2008; hooks, 2009), we propose this critical response cycle. Rather than being a prescription for what teachers "should always" do, we intend this cycle to be flexible and adaptable by teachers for their unique students, locations, and community needs. The cycle includes four phases: 1) identifying public artworks, 2) researching and interpreting, 3) responding with art, and 4) critiquing the response and planning future action.[1] These phases provide scaffolding for understanding complex and possibly contradictory meanings of public artworks. After discussing the four phases, we illustrate what this process might look like with two public art examples: Monument Avenue in Richmond, Virginia, and the Heidelberg Project in Detroit, Michigan.

Identifying the Art

In the first phase, student researchers inventory objects in the local environment they identify as public art.[2] This "mapping" of community art resources can literally use maps, drawing, or even digital technologies. This process, an elaboration of Kretzmann and McKnight's (1993) idea, could also involve students surveying and interviewing community members about public art in their city.

Researching and Interpreting

Students' understandings of public artworks are enhanced by knowledge of the time the work was created, the subject of the work, and how the work's meaning functions in the present day (Loewen, 1999). Thus, students can research historical and current events related to the public art they are studying. Interpreting the art in relation to a developing knowledge base about the artwork's history can generate a dynamic cycle in which initial interpretations may be revised and revisited. This research and interpretation phase lends itself to interdisciplinary possibilities where teachers might collaborate to combine resources and perspectives following Parsons's (2004) idea of local public art providing pathways to integrated curriculum. Further, this idea addresses Hutzel's (2007) call for the examination of collective identities in urban art education.

Responding with Art

Having researched the historical and present-day contexts of public artwork, students develop their own art as a response. Artistic responses to public art include paintings, sculptures, installations, performance pieces, transient or permanent additions to the site, signage, and craft bombing.[3] Teachers could help students conceptualize responses through brainstorming or other ideation exercises assisting students in locating salient aspects of the artwork. Further, students might create art to be performed or placed near the public artwork, "activating" both the student art and the public art.

Critiquing the Response and Planning Future Action

After creating response artworks, students should consider the functions and effects of their pieces. Interviewing local community members or inviting them to participate allows students and community members to think about their roles in creating and changing meanings. Below, we offer two examples of public art, one historical and one contemporary, and suggest how the critical response cycle might engage students in this public art.

INVESTIGATING PUBLIC ART THROUGH
THE CRITICAL RESPONSE CYCLE

Russell (2004) identified three types of public art: "Hero-on-a-Horse," "Form-and-Freedom," and "Collaborate-and-Create." In choosing our examples, the sculptures

on Monument Avenue in Richmond, Virginia, and the Heidelberg Project in Detroit, Michigan, we intentionally picked public artworks that exemplify opposite
ends of Russell's spectrum. The sculptures on Monument Avenue relate to Russell's
"Hero-on-a-Horse" category in their idealized and heroic depictions of Confederate leaders. The Heidelberg Project is an example of "Collaborate-and-Create" in
that it is an ongoing work of public art involving the artist and community, emphasizing dialogue and grass-roots community revitalization.[4]

Monument Avenue as a Potential Asset

> When I first moved to Richmond, I was stunned by the massive sculptures
> of Confederates on Monument Avenue. When I broached the topic of these
> sculptures and racism in the public landscape, many people responded with,
> "It's Richmond, what do you expect?"
> —Melanie Buffington, personal notes, 2010

Monument Avenue, a grand thoroughfare in Richmond, Virginia, is home
to five large statues commemorating Confederates. These are Richmond's most
prominent public artworks. The sculptures are enormous, heroic depictions
sculpted from granite and bronze, and they are a dominant narrative. Unexamined, the Confederate sculptures on Monument Avenue can act as agents of hegemony (see Figure 13.1). How could these public sculptures be an asset to students
in Richmond?

Identifying the Art

Richmond schoolchildren mapping public art resources in their city might identify the statues on Monument Avenue. In addition to drawing maps of these
sculptures, students can map the meaning of these works by recording personal
observations and stories about the monuments. Maybe the students have played
tag at the base of the Lee monument or seen people dressed in Civil War costumes
displaying Confederate flags—uses of the monument that create different meanings in the present. These two uses of the space create different meanings for the
sculpture, and students could map a variety of ways people use the public spaces.

Researching and Interpreting

After identifying the sculptures and mapping ways people use them, students
could research the men depicted, contemporaneous historical figures not me-
morialized on Monument Avenue, the time the monuments commemorate,

Figure 13.1. Monument Avenue.

when they were erected, and how they are understood today (Loewen, 1999). In "Hero-on-a-Horse" public art (Russell, 2004), the absence of certain figures speaks to knowledge repressed, as cultures tend to tell stories through monuments reinforcing the power of dominant groups. To learn about the history of the monuments, students might use historic archives, library research, and interviews with community members. Further, the teacher might invite guest speakers from local historical organizations, reenactors, or other groups that utilize the monuments. The research about the sculptures becomes a community endeavor involving an understanding of the complex past, present, and future meanings of the sculptures.

During this research, students should work to understand the multitude of meanings these sculptures have to different people. Students could also consider how Richmond's choice of commemorating Confederates with these sculptures in the early part of the 20th century contrasts with Richmond's contemporary choice to sculpturally memorialize Arthur Ashe, a Richmond-born tennis star and humanitarian. When investigating the history of Monument Avenue, students will likely learn about the Lost Cause era in which the monuments were erected, when there was a movement to re-remember the Civil War as a noble fight against Northern aggression in honor of states' rights, rather than to defend slavery. Comparing and contrasting the Lost Cause era to the present day would help students see how history is not fixed, how it changes over time, and how artworks intended to depict historical events are shaped by beliefs of the time they were made.

Responding with Art

The response phase includes the necessary action to unite critical pedagogy, participatory action research, and community development. Students can make art in response to what they learned about these sculptures; instigate important conversations in the community; bring attention to issues related to the sculptures; and add to, change, or support the meaning of the monuments to the community. For instance, a teacher might have students create drawings, scale models, or plans for remaking Monument Avenue with contemporary heroic figures. The students might work collaboratively to create a monument to a person or event relevant to their school. Or the students and teacher might involve others in the school and city in generating ideas for what they might create in order to change, reclaim, or renew the complex meanings of the sculptures.

Critiquing the Response and Planning Future Action

In the final phase, students critique their artistic responses, thinking about the new meanings they created. In this case, students address the Civil War, the Confederacy, the legacy of discrimination today, and contemporary issues of race and (in)equality. In addition to critiquing the art, students also reflect on their experience with the critical response cycle. If students created models or drawings for potential new art on Monument Avenue, they might evaluate the strengths of each idea and select a few to present to the city council. Alternatively, if students created an artistic intervention near a monument, they might interview people who interacted with their art to assess viewers' responses. Ideally, this reflection would lead to a cyclical process in which students' insights and knowledge could be applied to the next project. Thus, the monuments become an opportunity for urban students to critically research and respond in ways that combine history, art-making, community reactions, and action.

The Heidelberg Project as an Asset

> One day, I took a visiting art educator to see the Heidelberg Project. Much to our surprise and delight, we were serendipitously able to spend a few hours with the artist, Tyree Guyton. It was a magical experience to meet him and to hear him talk about the community revitalization central to the work.
> —Melanie Buffington, personal notes, 2010

In contrast to Monument Avenue, the Heidelberg Project is an ongoing, collaborative, change-oriented public art project with community at its core. Tyree Guyton started the Heidelberg Project in 1986 by cleaning his brushes on, and eventually painting on, the streets and abandoned houses of his East Detroit neighborhood on Heidelberg Street (Buffington, 2007). The project evolved as he used abandoned houses and abandoned objects including dolls, shoes, televisions, and car hoods as elements in a large artwork spanning several blocks on Heidelberg Street. With this project, he brings life and color to the neighborhood and calls attention to issues

Figure 13.2. The Heidelberg Project.

including homelessness, child abuse, unemployment, poverty, racial hatred, prostitution, and governmental failure. Although the city of Detroit demolished parts of the Heidelberg project in 1991 and again in 1999, Guyton continues to add to it, incorporating ongoing community involvement. The Heidelberg Project is now an organization that runs a summer camp involving children in the public artwork.

Identifying the Art

Students in Detroit who identify the Heidelberg Project when mapping public art resources in their city may map its physical location and add their personal experiences through writing stories, drawing pictures, or reflecting about their interactions with it.

Researching and Interpreting

In contrast to Monument Avenue, students who research contemporary works may be able to interview the artist. Thus, students might talk with Guyton or supporters and opponents of the Heidelberg Project who live nearby. Students might use newspaper articles as primary sources to learn about controversies over the project and its partial demolitions. Since the Heidelberg Project is intended to inspire action and dialogue, students could investigate other artworks in Detroit or elsewhere that were catalyzed by the Heidelberg Project.

Guyton's primary use of discarded objects leads some viewers to question the Heidelberg Project as art. Thus, interpreting this piece could bring up significant issues related to its meaning, the function of art in a public space, the connotations of everyday materials, and aesthetic concerns. Exploring these issues allows students to recognize more objects as public art in their community, such as yard art installations (Lai & Ball, 2002).

Responding with Art

Since the purpose of the Heidelberg Project *is* action, this presents a stark contrast to Monument Avenue. In the art-making phase, a class in Detroit might invite Tyree Guyton to work with students to imagine what they could add to the Heidelberg Project. Collaboratively, students could create art for the Heidelberg Project site or a satellite site at their school. Their art might be in direct response to Guyton's work, or they could use his ideas to inspire another artistic direction. Students could use digital media to document their research and artworks for distribution on the Internet.

Critiquing the Response and Planning Future Action

After creating responses to the Heidelberg Project, students should critically consider how their works added to the Heidelberg Project. This critique should address the role of artists in their city, how public art contributes to a community, and how student voices were represented through their addition to the Heidelberg Project. Thus, giving students the opportunity to critically interpret and act upon works of public art may help them see physical assets in their city while building a sense of community between the students and other community members.

URBAN ART AS A VEHICLE FOR CHANGE

The critical response cycle synthesizes elements of urban critical pedagogy, PAR, and ABCD to situate students as researchers, artists, and activists building their communities. We believe a uniform "cookie-cutter approach" to teaching is unlikely to be successful in a city. Thus, we purposefully designed the critical response cycle to be adaptable by teachers who know their students, their community, and their city's public art. Thus, teachers and students have the power to teach and learn in ways that resonate with them. In the critical response cycle, public art is a linchpin, securing the community-building process and acting as the medium through which change occurs. Students are situated as artists, researchers, and important assets in their communities, and their artwork becomes a response, a form of research, and a possible vehicle for change.

NOTES

1. It is not essential that the steps always occur in this order.
2. Ideally, the participants should be involved in identifying the assets to explore.
3. Craft bombing refers to a trend in which handmade craft items are used in artistic interventions, usually in the built environment.
4. In Russell's descriptions of these orientations to public art, he includes two subcategories for the larger "Collaborate-and-Create." The Heidelberg Project has aspects that relate to both the "Listen-and-Lead" subcategory as well as the "Confer-and-Defer" subcategory.

REFERENCES

Argiro, C. (2004). Teaching with public art. *Art Education, 57*(7), 23–32.
Buffington, M. L. (2007). Art to bring about change: The work of Tyree Guyton. *Art Education, 60*(4), 25–32.
Duncan-Andrade, J. M. R., & Morrell, E. (2008). *The art of critical pedagogy: Possibilities for moving from theory to practice in urban schools.* New York: Peter Lang Publishing.
Haney, W., & Lykes, M. B. (2010). Practice, participatory research and creative research designs. In W. Luttrell (Ed.), *Qualitative educational research: Readings in reflexive methodology and transformative practice* (pp. 108–122). New York: Routledge.

hooks, b. (2009). *Belonging: A culture of place.* New York: Routledge.

Hutzel, K. (2007). Reconstructing a community, reclaiming a playground: A participatory action research study. *Studies in Art Education, 48*(3), 299–315.

Kretzmann, J. P., & McKnight, J. L. (1993). *Building communities from the inside out: A path toward finding and mobilizing a community's assets.* Chicago, IL: ACTA Publications.

Lai, A., & Ball, E. (2002). Home is where the art is: Exploring the places people live through art education. *Studies in Art Education, 44*(1), 47–66.

Loewen, J. W. (1999). *Lies across America: What our historic sites get wrong.* New York: The New Press.

Parsons, M. (2004). Art and integrated curriculum. In E. W. Eisner & M. D. Day (Eds.), *Handbook of research and policy in art education* (pp. 775–794). Mahwah, NJ: Lawrence Erlbaum Associates.

Russell, R. (2004). A beginner's guide to public art. *Art Education, 57*(4), 19–24.

Conclusion

FLÁVIA M. C. BASTOS, KIM COSIER, AND KAREN HUTZEL

> When, in relation to a given subject, science has neither a precise explanation nor unquestionable knowledge, the way is open for poetic interpretation.
> —Augusto Boal, *The Aesthetics of the Oppressed*

Art is the kind of human cultural endeavor capable of capturing the complexity and cacophony of the city, rendering it meaningful to the diverse students who live in cities and participate in urban schools. Our examination and advocacy for a reimagined urban school that is grounded in art education represent collective and critical voices of resistance and ownership. As such, we challenge narrowly defined and corrupt notions of urban schooling and education that denigrate urban youth by demanding subservience and denying their humanity. Echoing Boal's activist views and reflecting contemporary artistic practices, we have proposed a conceptualization of urban schools through an asset-based framework that includes counternarratives, social capital mapping, cultural and artistic production that is integrated across the curriculum, and social inquiry and critique.

Our work proposes a departure from reductionist understandings of urban school phenomena. Likewise, we propose a detour away from outdated (but still prevalent) art education and general education practices that have little connection to contemporary youth. We argue for a move toward a teaching praxis based on place-based pedagogy and the work of contemporary artists, who often turn conventional wisdom on its head and create new ways of making meaning. Art engages humans in meaning-making processes to explore, imagine, and criticize life as they know and live it. Our reimagination of education through art insists on such engagement because we believe, as Boal (2006) affirms, that "to live, to exercise our power and occupy our territory, we humans . . . need to perceive the world in which we live" (p. 34). Throughout this book, authors seek to develop new poetics of urban education wedded to the possibility of reinvesting urban school experiences with impending success of education through art.

By focusing on the assets present in school communities and by mining the city for inspiration and culturally relevant curricular content, we honor the knowledge of students, families, and neighbors. In our view, reimagining urban education through art insists on developing a pedagogy that capitalizes on the cultural knowledge city dwellers possess and asks them to be drivers of their own education. Such approaches also honor urban students because "art and art integration simply make classrooms and schools more desirable places to be" (Noblit, Corbett, Wilson, & McKinney, 2009, p. 1).

Transforming the school into a site of neighborhood renewal is part of our vision. In this paradigm, schools become drivers of change in neighborhoods that have sometimes been written off by both insiders and outsiders. We believe an education that seriously considers urban visualities and the assets of the city and its inhabitants as fitting content for intellectual endeavor holds promise for our future. Current talk of urban renewal and new urbanism frequently hails the arts as pivotal in creating desirable communities and recognizes that urban spaces hold untapped potential for development. Adding to this discourse, we seek to centrally position education in this timely discussion about urban development. Challenging rampant mainstream views of urban spaces as disadvantaged, the authors of the book's first part focus on *assets* to examine the educational and artistic potential of cities.

The first part of this book promotes an understanding of the city as a social, cultural, and educational asset. We invite educators to be inspired by contemporary and historical art practices that celebrate an archetypical and intangible notion of city and use it as a foundation for place-based transformative pedagogies. We honor complexity, understanding that cities range from cosmopolitan and electrifying, as in New York or San Francisco, to mid-sized Midwest varieties of empty and/or segregated urban cores and sprawling suburbs, such as Detroit and Milwaukee. Nevertheless, cities are not only a shared dimension of our globalized experiences, they also embed paramount human attempts at social order, and have throughout their development welcomed and relied upon innovative artistic and scientific solutions to develop, grow, and remain vibrant. The theoretical frameworks outlined in the book's first part honor a city poetics and share optimistic views of education that conceive of schools and art practices as central to creating and sustaining vital city neighborhoods.

Collectively, these authors' voices contribute to a cartography of change and possibility that builds on existing assets. These assets include women who historically leveraged their position to gain the right to fully participate in decisions affecting their own lives, and, as Funk describes, the ways in which they have "troubled," challenged, and ultimately transformed "Weber's social closure mechanisms." They also include the diverse and frequently neglected *voices* and perspectives *of students of color* that Whitehead proposes can be heard through "counterstorytelling" practices in education and in art. Bastos's persuasion for "seeing the city" with all it offers is a condition to begin the process of empowering urban communities to build upon and negotiate access to resources, including a good-quality education. The path outlined here has the potential to inspire contemporary and transgressive education practices that dare to "rewrite the imagination in the service of a new critical imaginary," as Weiner (2007, p. 69) suggests, in which the city is a site of excellence for learning about and with the arts.

In the book's second part we focused on teacher education and professional development because we believe that the sort of educational transformation we advocate for is a complex endeavor that must be supported in purposeful ways. The chapters in Part II explore three common, broad areas of knowledge: Understanding self through purposeful reflection on the social construction of identity; understanding diverse learners through community-building; and understanding cultural complexity through engagement with theory and practice.

In each chapter, people who chose to pursue a life in teaching were asked to reflect upon the construction of their own identity as they engaged in teaching in the city. Such self-reflective practices inculcate habits of mind that challenge entrenched ways of thinking about identity and cultural difference, interrogate accepted but unexamined ideas about schooling, and spark the individual's social imagination.

In order to address how we come to understand diverse learners, the part's authors stressed the importance of creating ways for teachers and future teachers to come to know and care about community members. Through various means, undergraduate and graduate students were prepared to learn from the city dwellers with whom they worked. Each chapter recounts processes involved in forging partnerships with the local community and leveraging the assets community members bring to the processes of collaboration. Each also addressed ways programs aim at helping students recognize the social factors that impinge on learners in urban settings, in order to better prepare teachers to understand the institutional and social factors that support and undermine urban children and youth.

Each chapter in the part addressed the importance of understanding cultural complexity. This complexity is comprised of negative factors, such as underfunded schools, segregation, and institutionalized racism, as well as positive factors, such as the artistic traditions of Guimarães's "culturally quilted territory" and Martin Luther King's "beloved community," about which Olivia Gude speaks. Such an approach to teaching insists on mining the city for curriculum and coming to know the particular challenges as well as the promise the city holds.

A binding factor across all chapters activating accounts of teacher education and professional development was the importance of faculty members deeply engaged in the educational process, modeling for their students ways of being in the city that hoped for a better future while drawing from the culturally rich resources of the present. For each of the authors, such engagement took on different dimensions, accounting for local contexts, specific populations, and the complex nature of this work.

Possibilities for enacting an asset-based approach to education in the city are endless. The complex and multifaceted pedagogies offered in this book's third part suggest ideas and possibilities that teachers might consider in repositioning art as central to meaningful and successful urban education practices. The asset-based foundation for each chapter highlights the potential and promise of urban youth and the cities where they live and go to school. Common factors in the pedagogies offered in this book include engaging children in collaborative efforts focused on local communities while honoring their ideas, opinions, and voices. Making education relevant to urban youths' lives, without devaluing or denigrating those realities, but rather celebrating and honoring them, makes a significant statement about society's values. The pedagogies presented in this book recognize and celebrate assets including (1) the children as important members of the community; (2) local arts and culture such as public art, museums, theaters, and galleries; (3) local adults such as artists, activists, and educators; (4) local institutions such as universities, churches, and museums; (5) city landscapes, buildings, streets, and parks; and (6) the art and culture produced by the students themselves. Through exploration, investigation, critique, and artistic production, urban students can immerse themselves in the richness, diversity, and complexity of the cities in which they live. Example curricula offered in this book can engage students in exploring and critiquing local public art and spaces they determine as sacred. They can work together toward a common goal, learning to see themselves and one another as significant members of the community. Students can curate museums celebrating and teaching about the culture they actively produce and experience. They can shoot photographs, produce video, and tell stories to communicate the complex realities of their lives and their cities. Students can stand up for a cause and educate adults on an issue. Such asset-based approaches can engage children in inhabiting their cities and their lives, and prepare them for 21st-century living.

Ultimately, our discussion of a city-focused educational theory, teacher preparation practices, and critical pedagogy grounded in arts conspires to transform prevalent views of urban education. Central to social justice concerns, urban schools remain redlined as sites of substandard education for disposable students.

The idea we have instilled throughout this book is that while bad schools contribute to undesirable cities, good schools are important in creating more just and livable ones. Furthermore, the ailments of public urban education can no longer be repaired with past approaches that bring about a reductionist curriculum, increased regimentation, and an overreliance on test scores that devalues creative teaching. City schools represent a timely challenge to be thoroughly and seriously considered. As the world grows increasingly diverse and urban, robust schools and educational practices that promote more just societies are at the center of our democratic ideals. As we have mapped in this volume, contemporary art practices and artists can contribute a model for reimagining and subsequently transforming city schools. If the arts are deemed to have potential to transform and enliven cities around the world, what could they do for public city schools? We hope to have presented ways in which city education can serve the public interest so that school communities are empowered to "further democracy, democratic practices, and social justice" (Banks, 2006, p. 141) through an artful, joyful, and equitable education that can sustain our cities.

REFERENCES

Banks, J. (2006). Democracy, diversity, and social justice: Educating citizens for the public interest in a global age. In G. Landson-Billings & W. F. Tate (Eds.), *Education research in the public interest: Social justice, action and policy* (pp. 141–157). New York: Teachers College Press.
Boal, A. (2006). *The aesthetics of the oppressed.* New York: Routledge.
Noblit, G. W., Corbett, H. D., Wilson, B. L., & McKinney, M. B. (2009). *Creating and sustaining arts-based school reform: the A+ Schools Program.* New York: Routledge.
Weiner, E. J. (2007). Critical pedagogy and the crisis of imagination. In P. McLaren & J. L. Kincheloe (Eds.), *Critical pedagogy: Where are we now?* (pp. 57–77). New York: Peter Lang.

Appendix:
The Unit Plans

UNIT PLAN I

UNIT TITLE: WORKING TOGETHER:
LOCAL COLLABORATIVE ART

(by Karen Hutzel)

Collaborative Public Art

Unit Goals

Students will identify, research, investigate, and honor local environmental assets through the creation and display of collaborative art.

City Assets

Local environment, school and the grounds, students, teachers, administrators, community members and artists, neighborhood organizations and groups.

Essential Questions

1. What environmental assets are important to us in our community?
2. How can we honor local environmental assets by working together?
3. What assets can we each contribute to our collaboration?

Activities

Identifying Local (Environmental) Assets: Students identify environmental assets in their community that are important to them through Internet and printed research, interviews with community members, discussion, community mapping, photography, and teacher generated ideas.
Engaging with the Local: Students choose a topic or focus to begin their research and inquiry, such as local recycling, ducks and sound, local architecture,

waterways, or trees. They involve teachers, community members, and local organizations to learn more about the topic.

Collaborative Art Planning: Students brainstorm with the involvement of teachers, community members, and artists for collaborative artwork(s). Plans are made for dividing up the work toward completion of the artwork. Small groups can be formed to lead particular tasks or complete particular sections of the artwork. The teacher or lead artist should facilitate this process to ensure equity and address conflicts.

Completion and Celebration: Students complete the artwork with the goal of displaying it permanently somewhere in the school or community. They finish the project with a celebration event.

UNIT PLAN 2

UNIT TITLE: SEEING SCHOOL "THROUGH STUDENTS' EYES"

(by Kristien Zenkov and Kimberly Sheridan)

Photography, Writing, Literacy

Unit Goals

Using photography and words, students will investigate their relationships to school in dialogic, collaborative inquiry with their teachers.

City Assets

Students' investigation into their ambivalent or negative experiences and/or attitudes toward school and how they might change these. Students' assets in their lives that may be previously unknown to their teachers.

Essential Questions

1. What are the purposes of school?
2. What helps you to succeed in school?
3. What gets in the way of your school success?

Activities

After an initial introduction to the project and instruction in the basics of photography, students participate in a "photo walk" in and around their school and local community. After a class discussion of the photographs taken on the photo walk, students then independently shoot a few dozen digital images in response to one of the project's essential questions. Through a one-on-one conversation with a teacher about their images, the students select an image that best conveys their thinking about each question. The image then serves as a launching point to write about how it relates to their thinking about the question. One-on-one writing conferences support the development of students' artistic interpretations and writing. This process is repeated for each essential question until a student has a set of three images and paragraphs that represent their thinking about their relationships to school.

UNIT PLAN 3

UNIT TITLE: CREATING PUBLIC SERVICE ANNOUNCEMENTS ON SOCIAL ISSUES

(by Mindi Rhoades)

Social Issues, Public Relations, Digital Video Skills

Unit Goals

Students will review, understand, analyze, write, produce, edit, and present original public service announcements (PSAs) about contemporary social justice issues while learning digital video skills.

City Assets

Government and social service agencies, interest groups and organizations, libraries, community members, local video artists, local video and arts venues.

Essential Questions

1. What important issues face our community, and what is their impact?
2. What do people need to know and do about these issues?
3. How do we communicate and measure the effectiveness of our messages?

Activities

Introducing the PSA: Students view, discuss, and analyze PSA examples.
Identifying Topics: Students brainstorm and select contemporary social justice issues impacting their communities.

Researching: Students do initial research using multimedia resources. Students also contact community members and organizations to locate and access additional relevant resources and information.

Crafting the Message: Students transform their issues into focused messages. They draft, share, edit, and revise any texts and/or narration needed.

Storyboarding: Students draft and revise visual outlines of their PSAs.

Making the PSA: Students learn and apply video and filmmaking skills while filming PSA footage.

Viewing and Analyzing: Students share and critique PSAs on content, form, and technical aspects. Students revise PSAs after feedback.

Displaying Publicly: Students screen and distribute their PSAs for different audiences: schools, community groups, local access television stations, the Internet, and local arts/movie venues.

Synthesizing: Students reflect on the process, final products, audience responses, potential impact, and their own learning and development.

UNIT PLAN 4

UNIT TITLE: CREATING A TEEN MUSEUM

(by Carol Ng-He)

Museums and Space

Unit Goals

To engage teens in conceptualizing and making museum exhibits reflecting "teen culture"; to empower teens by giving them ownership of a cultural institution through collaboration, active leadership, creative programmatic planning and participation; to invigorate the city with teens' artistic contributions in a teen-oriented museum context.

City Assets

The city as curriculum: Using social issues identified by teens, they can turn them into potential exhibit themes for the Chicago Teen Museum. The city as resource: The CTM continues to build partnerships with other local museums and schools to implement programs for teens to create art projects concerning teen culture. Teens giving back to the city: CTM programs aim to nurture teens to be the mentors for future teens. The CTM also offers to be a resource hub for other scholars, museum professionals, educators, parents, policymakers, and peers of teens in understanding the multiple facets of teen culture.

Essential Questions

1. How can teens' schools/neighborhoods/communities/organizations help shape who they think they are?
2. How does the history of any or all of these places inform teens about their identity and connect to their future aspirations?
3. How can schools provide resources to bring museums into their classrooms?
4. How do teens interpret teen culture?
5. What is the importance for the city, and teens, to recognize teen culture now and in the future?

Art/Artist/Visual Culture Examples

Anne Frank, Joseph Cornell, Buckminster Fuller, John Hughes, Olafur Eliasson.

Activities

After-school Teen Council meetings in which a group of teens convene and discuss aspects of teen culture as to help to develop potential future exhibit and programming ideas for a teen museum; a website advisory in which veterans from the Teen Council and new members provide advices to the teen museum in making the virtual presence of the organization appealing to teens from different places; teens' contribution and facilitation on blogs in which teens from everywhere could exchange ideas online, discussing the topics and issues concerning teen culture.

UNIT PLAN 5

UNIT TITLE: "SACRED STRUCTURES"— A UNIT WITHIN THE THEMATIC STUDY OF "ME AND MY COMMUNITY"

(by James Haywood Rolling Jr.)

Three-Dimensional Model-Making

Unit Goals

Students will investigate the architecture of sacred buildings in the local community, along with the practices and traditions celebrated there. Students will design and construct a three-dimensional model of a structure to house a self-selected sacred activity.

City Assets

Religious buildings; sacred spaces; diversity of youth perspectives.

Essential Questions

1. What are some of the things we do or some of the places we go that are so very special, we call them sacred?
2. What makes them sacred to us?
3. What activity is special enough for me to build my own sacred structure to practice it in?
4. How would I describe some of the different parts (or shapes, or numbers, or colors used) that make up my sacred structure? What does each of them symbolize?

Activities

Students map and model the structure of their school building, then investigate neighborhood architecture and ultimately examine the symbols and customs connected to local religious buildings and cultural traditions. Students identify a practice so special to them, they define it as sacred. Students will then design and construct a three-dimensional model of a structure to house that sacred practice. Begin with a worksheet activity prompted by essential questions, dialogue about student responses, presentations on the vocabulary of building forms as symbols, and project sketches. The unit concludes with the student design of unique characteristics to surround their sacred functions, and ultimately with the facilitated construction of their own architectural models.

UNIT PLAN 6

UNIT TITLE: UNDERSTANDING AND RESPONDING TO PUBLIC ART

(by Melanie Buffington and Erin Waldner)

Public Art, Collaborative Art-Making

Unit Goals

Students will identify, understand, respond to, and possibly reclaim local works of public art. Students will learn about the histories and identities present in their own cities and neighborhoods.

City Assets

Local works of public art, local artists, community members, students, historical societies, museums, art councils, neighborhood groups, newspaper archives.

Essential Questions

1. Why are public artworks important to a community?
2. What do public artworks say about a community?
3. How do public artworks represent or misrepresent community identities?

Activities

Identifying the Art: Students go into their neighborhoods and map sanctioned and unsanctioned public art. Students work together to create a visual map.

Researching and Interpreting: Students choose a work of public art from the map. In groups, students do research on the public art to enhance the visual map. Students utilize the maps toward interpreting and developing their understandings of the meaning(s) of the public art.

Responding with Art: Students create their own artworks in response to the public art by making site-specific art or proposals for new works of public art. Exhibit the art either in an official exhibition venue or unofficially near the public art.

Critiquing the Response and Planning Future Action: Invite members of the community (including artists) to join in interpreting the students' artistic responses. Students reflect on how their artwork functioned. Students plan for future research and art-making.

Glossary of Terms

action research. research in collaboration with participants with the intent to create change, often done in schools or organizations to improve practices and results.

artivism. artistic interventions; activism through the arts.

asset-based education. encompasses education practices and perspectives that build on the possibilities existing in various school communities, including individual, interpersonal, environmental, cultural, artistic, historical, and material assets. In direct opposition to a needs-based focus, asset-based education seeks to indentify, nourish, and build upon these assets to create sustainable educational models.

asset-based community development. an approach for community development and organizing that draws upon neighborhoods' existing assets; an innovative strategy for community-driven development utilized in both urban neighborhoods and rural communities.

asset-based planning. community and educational planning driven by social assets: the particular talents of individuals, as well as the social capital inherent in the relationships that fuel local associations and informal networks.

built environment. human-made surroundings providing sites for human activities; a physical, spatial and cultural product.

community. a fluid and expansive network of relationships; ecology; a geographic location with set boundaries.

community-based art. artistic practices that seek to improve life conditions and empower residents of a particular community, typically involving partnerships and various levels of collaboration/negotiation.

community development. practices that improve dimensions of a local community, including building local capacity through skill development.

constructivist learning. pedagogical approach based on cognitive psychology's understandings of students' process of generating knowledge that puts a premium on active engagement, including investigating, exploring, and criticizing.

counternarrative. self-empowerment language developed and based on authentic perspectives that aim to cast doubt on the validity of accepted premises or myths, especially the ones held by the majority.

craft bombing. a trend in which handmade craft items are used in artistic interventions, usually in the built environment.

critical pedagogy. an educational theory and teaching/learning practice designed to raise learners' critical consciousness, ability to articulate their own position in the world, awareness of social mechanisms of oppression, and capacity to affect change.

critical race theory. originated as a radical legal movement that holds racism as the norm in United States society. As a broader scholarly tradition, CRT denounces the limits of reform initiatives, such as the Civil Rights Movement, affirmative action, and multiculturalism in schools. It seeks to challenge the status quo by using narratives of those typically excluded to transform relationships and understandings about race, racism, and power.

critical response cycle. engaging students in understanding, reclaiming, and adding new meanings to existing structures; provides scaffolding for understanding complex and contradictory meanings of public artworks.

critical theory. theory intended to go beyond understanding or explaining, toward creating change in society.

culturally relevant pedagogy. learning about and through issues important/relevant to learners, inspiring sophisticated, complex perspectives in critically examining *their* concerns.

democracy. a form of government that is governed by the people and in which the majority rules. For Dewey, and for us, democracy is also an ethical ideal, a personal commitment to participatory civic engagement.

discipline-based art education. an art education reform that gained popularity in the 1980s with funding from the Getty Center for Education in the Arts. This approach promotes education across four disciplines: aesthetics (ideas about the nature of art), art criticism (bases for judging art), art history (contexts in which art has been created), and art production (gaining skill in processes and techniques for creating art).

education organizing. a new branch of community organizing seeking to make schools more responsive to community needs, advocating bottom-up changes and based on developing power and trust in urban neighborhoods.

hegemony. authority, control, or dominant influence held by one person/group, often upheld by both the oppressors and oppressed.

heterosexual norms/heteronormativity. terms used to describe and critique the way institutions and policies reinforce certain beliefs about gender and sexuality, which includes the belief that human beings fall into two distinct categories, male and female; that sexual and marital relations are normal only between two people of different genders; and that each gender has certain natural roles in life.

homogeneous. similar or of the same kind; having uniform structure or composition.

literacy. the ability to create and decode meaning in various forms of human communication, including art.

LGBTQ. Lesbian, Gay, Bisexual, Transgender, and Queer/Questioning.

marginalization. a downgrade or confinement to a low standing or outer edge in social standing.

misogyny. a dislike or hatred of women.

multicultural education. a multifaceted teaching strategy that recognizes the pluralistic nature of society; intended to promote democracy and positive self-concept across multiple cultural identifiers.

neo-Marxist. describes social theory and sociological analysis that draws on and extends the ideas of Karl Marx to examine political and economic systems.

No Child Left Behind Act (NCLB). standards-based education reform, based on the concept of setting standards and goals to improve education.

participatory action research. research method (using critical theory) used by educators involved in change-oriented work toward social justice; the researcher conducts the study with the participants rather than on the participants.

photovoice. a method of action research that combines photography with grass-roots social action.

praxis. involves a process of action-reflection-action that is central to the development of a consciousness of power and how it operates; in educational discourse it typically refers to the process of engaging in transformative school practices guided by critical pedagogy and research.

public art. artwork intended for the exhibition or display in a public space.

resilience theory. theory that explains ways by which individuals develop an ability to cope in times of adversity.

sacred sites. the term "sacred" is an activity, belief, or object one considers so special that one might build a structure devoted to practicing, recognizing, or preserving it.

segregation. to separate or isolate one thing or person from another and place in a separate group; in education, segregation is usually associated with race.

service learning. a methodology of collaborative learning focused on civic engagement as a curricular approach to teaching subject matter.

social contract (of school). agreement of *social* rights, duties, and responsibilities of the parties involved, usually members of the society.

social justice. a concept in which everyone deserves and works toward equal rights and opportunities, i.e., economic, political, and social.

social reconstruction. a level of multicultural education that engages students in seeking social justice and change.

teen museum. a museum dedicated to the preservation of teen culture.

urban imaginary. the cognitive and somatic image we carry within us of the places where we live, work, and play.

visual culture. concept that focuses on aspects of culture that rely on visual images and their interpretations.

visual literacy. one's ability to interpret and create meaning from an image; an idea that images can be "read" and meaning from these images can be communicated.

Online Resources

Arts Education Partnership:
http://www.aep-arts.org/

Barefoot Artists:
http://www.barefootartists.org/index.html

Educator's Network for Social Justice:
http://www.ensj.org/

Faith Quilts Project:
http://www.huntalternatives.org/pages/106_the_faith_quilts_project.cfm

The Freire International Project for Critical Pedagogy:
http://freireproject.org/

GLSEN Gay, Lesbian, Straight Educator's Network:
http://www.glsen.org/cgi-bin/iowa/all/home/index.html

National Art Education Association:
www.naea-reston.org

New York Collective of Radical Educators:
http://www.nycore.org/

No Name Gallery:
http://www.soapfactory.org/

Rethinking Schools:
http://www.rethinkingschools.org/index.shtml

Teachers for Social Justice:
http://www.teachersforjustice.org/

Teaching Tolerance:
www.tolerance.org

Village of the Arts and Humanities:
http://www.villagearts.org/programs.htm

About the Editors and the Contributors

The Editors

Flávia M. C. Bastos is a Brazilian native who lives and works in the United States. She directs the School of Art and coordinates the Art at the University of Cincinnati, where she also directs the Art in the Market Program, a community-based initiative that teams local youth and students from the College of Design, Architecture, Art and Planning to improve neighborhoods and empower participants through the process of community art. Her scholarship is indebted to her Brazilian roots and experiences with social and cultural diversity and inspired by the educational philosophy of educator Paulo Freire. Growing up in an urban environment, Bastos benefited from the opportunities a public and free education afforded her during the entirety of her schooling (K–higher education). During her lifetime she has witnessed the decline of public education in her home country and faced surprise, disbelief, and anger at finding urban schools in the United States to be on a par with the inner-city schools where she worked in the Third World. As a parent of a bicultural child, Bastos faced many adventures in the pursuit of a quality education for her daughter. Her scholarship, teaching, and service are fueled by a commitment to engender transformative educational practices that honor the artistic potential and celebrate the possibilities and talents of all people.

Kim Cosier is the head of art education at the University of Wisconsin–Milwaukee (UWM). She is co-founder, with Laura Trafí-Prats, of the Milwaukee Visionaries Project, a media literacy/video production and animation project for middle and high school youth. Her scholarship focuses on art education for social justice, alternative education, and other intervention programs for at-risk youth, and on LGBTQ issues in education. Doing this research is a labor of love, since UWM is an urban, public university and struggles with many of the same challenges that face urban, public elementary and secondary schools. Dr. Cosier's interests in championing the underdog also come from her own experiences, being raised by parents whose religious beliefs led the family into an unconventional life that often prompted scorn from teachers and schoolmates alike. Growing up strangely gave Cosier an outsider perspective that turns out to be beneficial when working with young people who don't fit in. Being queer provided an escape from torment by ensuring that she left behind the unforgiving farm town where she went to middle and high school to make a life for herself in more civilized urban places. Cosier now lives happily in Milwaukee's Riverwest neighborhood with her wife, Josie, and their dogs Jack and Evie Mae.

Karen Hutzel is assistant professor and director of the Mostly Online M.A. Degree Program in Art Education at The Ohio State University in Columbus, Ohio. Through an action research approach, she has explored topics such as service learning, community arts, and social reconstruction. Similar to many teachers today, Hutzel grew up in a suburban, predominately White community, unaware of social injustices that provided her with privileges she didn't necessarily recognize as a working-class kid surrounded by more economically privileged classmates. Seeking culturally diverse experiences to contribute to social change, she realized and challenged her own savior mentality while developing public community art pieces with urban youth in some of the poorest neighborhoods in Cincinnati, Ohio. These children taught her the significance of community, of cultural expression and relevance, and of their plight in dilapidated urban schools. Since becoming a college educator of future art teachers, she has maintained involvement with urban children through service learning activities founded on collaborative models of art-making, further challenging her students' privileges toward seeking empathic understandings and social action. She earned her B.F.A. from the University of Dayton, her M.A. from the University of Cincinnati, and her Ph.D. from Florida State University. She lives in Columbus, Ohio, with her husband, Ricky, stepdaughter, Brianna, and dogs, Saka and Sophie.

The Contributors

Sharif Bey is a dual assistant professor in art education and teaching and leadership at Syracuse University. He grew up in the city of Pittsburgh and has worked extensively in urban schools. In addition to being an active teacher and scholar, he continues to exhibit his sculptures nationally and internationally.

Bryna Bobick is assistant professor of art education at the University of Memphis. She has given professional presentations, both locally and nationally, on the topics of urban education, curriculum development, and museum partnerships with the community. She is a former elementary art teacher in Georgia and is a practicing studio artist.

Melanie Buffington is currently an assistant professor of art education at Virginia Commonwealth University. She is a former middle school art teacher who graduated from Penn State University (B.S.) and The Ohio State University (M.A.,

Ph.D.). Her current research interests include teacher preparation, multicultural-ism, social justice, technology, museum education, and contemporary art.

Clayton Funk is assistant professor of art education at The Ohio State University. His research on cultural history of art education appears in research journals, book chapters, and his book, *Contemporary Art Culture* (2009, 2nd ed.). Funk received his doctorate in art education from Teachers College, Columbia University.

Olivia Gude is a professor at the University of Illinois at Chicago and the founding director of Spiral Workshop. She has received many awards and commissions as an art educator and for her collaborative public artwork, including two National Endowment for the Arts Art in Public Places awards and the 2009 Lowenfeld Award from the National Art Education Association.

Leda Guimarães is professor of art education at the Federal University of Goiás (Brazil), where she works in undergraduate and graduate programs that focus on teacher education, art, and visual culture. Her research engages art education, visual culture, and critical pedagogy in schools and community sites. Guimarães is vice president of the FAEB, a federal association of art educators in Brazil, and is one of three art educators chosen to represent InSea in Latin America for 2011/2012 period. She was a visiting scholar in the Art Education Department of The Ohio State University during her doctoral studies.

Donalyn Heise is associate professor of art education at the University of Memphis. Her research includes instructional technology for art teacher preparation, resilience theory, and community art collaborations in urban settings. She has received numerous grants and awards, and has conducted over 100 workshops and presentations at the state, regional, and national levels.

Carol Ng-He, born and raised in Hong Kong, received an M.A. in art education from the School of the Art Institute of Chicago. Carol serves as Education Director at Intuit: The Center for Intuitive and Outsider Art and Program Developer at Chicago Teen Museum. Carol is an adjunct faculty member at Columbia College Chicago.

Mindi Rhoades is a visiting professor in The Ohio State University's College of Education. Her research interests include LGBTQ issues and education, social justice, arts-based learning, visual culture, meaning-making, classroom dramatic inquiry, and embodied learning. Her work with Youth Video OUTreach allowed her to apply all of these.

James Haywood Rolling Jr. earned his Ed.D. in art education at Teachers College, Columbia University, and his M.F.A. in studio arts research from Syracuse

University. His research interests include arts-based research, urban education, and narrative inquiry. Dr. Rolling is associate professor and chair of art education at Syracuse University.

Kimberly Sheridan is an assistant professor of educational psychology and art education at George Mason University, where she researches learning and cognition in arts and media. She earned her doctorate from Harvard University's Graduate School of Education, and has received National Science Foundation, Spencer Foundation, and Fulbright grants and awards.

Erin Waldner is a graduate student in the Art Education Department at Virginia Commonwealth University, where she is working toward teaching licensure. Her graduate research has focused on issues surrounding public art and monuments, and how critical pedagogy can be used to address these in public school and community settings.

Jessie L. Whitehead is the graduate coordinator of art education at Southern Connecticut State University. Her primary area of research is artists outside the margins, which includes women artists and artists of color. Two of her research articles are "The Invisibility of Blackness" and "Theorizing Experience: Four Women Artists of Color."

Kristien Zenkov is associate professor of education at George Mason University and co-director of Through Students' Eyes, which asks diverse youth to document their perceptions of school with photographs and writing. He has published more than 70 articles, book chapters, and books concerning teacher education and literacy.

Index

Collaborative art learning, 95–101
  common practices in, 98
  models, 98–101
  multiculturalism and, 95–96
  public art, unit plan for, 153–154
  service learning and, 97–98
  student engagement/re-engagement
    through, 96–98, 101
  unit plan for, 158–159
Collaborative for Education
  Organizing, 22n1
Collage, city as (Gude-Cosier
  dialogue), 81–82
Collier, K. G., 96
Collins, A., 114
Collins, G., 49
Comber, B., 76
Community
  arts projects based in, 20–21, 63–66
  assets, connecting art pedagogy to,
    83–85
  author experiences, 91–94
  changing perspectives of LGBTQ
    youth in, 116
  curriculum based on needs of,
    service learning and, 74–76
  Gude-Cosier dialogue on, 80–90
  school's relationship with, 31
  student-led research in, 62–66
  understanding of, 21
Community Arts Academy, Memphis,
  TN
  curriculum and instructional style, 73
  neighborhood demographics, 72–73
  new teacher experiences, 73–74
  teacher preparation and, goals of,
    75–76
Community-based organizations
  (CBOs), 119–120
Community outreach, Youth Video
  OUTreach (YVO) project and,
  119–120

Community work
  education organizing and, 16, 22n1
  parental involvement and, 31
Concealed stories, 36, 37
Condit, C. W., 25
Condon, D., 103
Connection-making, 125
Constructivist art studio project,
  129–136
Cook-Sather, A., 103
"Cool cities" strategy, 18
Cooper, J., & Associates, 96
Cooper, M., 97
Cooper, N., 71
Coral Shores High School, Florida,
  collaborative art learning in,
  98–99
Corbett, H. D., 149
Corker, M., 53
Cosier, K., 43, 47, 49, 148
  Olivia Gude and, dialogue between,
    80–90
Counternarratives, of artists of color,
  34–41
Counterstorytellers, contemporary,
  37–38
Counterstorytelling
  and critical race theory, 36–37
  defined, 36
  origins, 35
  as transformative opportunity, 35–36
  types, 36–37
  urban art education and, 38–39
  visual narratives as, 38
Cowan, C. P., 71
Cowan, P. A., 71
Creative class, city renewal and, 18
Critical consciousness, developing,
  115–117
Critical pedagogy
  critical response cycle and, 146
  teacher education and, 49–50